Meet the Siberian Husky

- The Siberian Husky is a member of the American Kennel Club's Working Group of dogs.

- Siberian Huskies were developed as sled dogs by the Chukchi tribe of northeast Asia and made their way to Alaska in the early 1900s.

- The word "husky" is actually the generic term the Chukchi tribe used to describe a "sled pulling dog."

- The Siberian Husky is also known as a Nordic dog. He shares his ancestry with the Alaskan Malamute and Samoyed.

- The Siberian Husky innately loves to work in large teams due to his mushing history. The heavier the Chukchis' sleds became, the more dogs the hunters would add to the team.

- Siberian Huskies are very outgoing, fun-loving animals.

- The Husky requires an enormous amount of exercise and physical activity.

- The Husky's double coat does not take much time or effort to groom, although you might have to clean up after his shedding hair quite often.

- The Siberian Husky comes in an array of beautiful colors including red and white, black and white, and silver and white.

Consulting Editor

IAN DUNBAR PH.D., MRCVS

Featuring Photographs by
dogphoto.com

Howell Book House

An Imprint of Macmillan General Reference USA
A Pearson Education Macmillan Company
1633 Broadway
New York, NY 10019

Library of Congress Cataloging-in-Publication
Data
The essential Siberian husky/consulting editor,
Ian Dunbar; featuring photographs by Kerrin
Winter and Dale Churchill.
        p.   cm.
  Includes bibliographical references and index.
  ISBN 1-58245-071-4
  1. Siberian Husky. I. Dunbar, Ian.
  SF429.S65E77 1999   99-24335
  636.76—dc21   CIP

Manufactured in the United States of America
10 9 8 7 6 5 4 3

Series Director: Michele Matrisciani
Production Team: David Faust, Marie Kristine
  Parial-Leonardo, Carol Sheehan
Book Design: Paul Costello
Photography: All photos by dogphoto.com

ARE YOU READY?!

☐ Have you prepared your home and your family for your new pet?

☐ Have you gotten the proper supplies you'll need to care for your dog?

☐ Have you found a veterinarian that you (and your dog) are comfortable with?

☐ Have you thought about how you want your dog to behave?

☐ Have you arranged your sched-ule to accommodate your dog's needs for exercise and attention?

No matter what stage you're at with your dog—still thinking about get-ting one, or he's already part of the family—this Essential guide will provide you with the practical infor-mation you need to understand and care for your canine companion. Of course you're ready—you have this book!

THE ESSENTIAL

Siberian Husky

The Siberian Husky's Senses

SIGHT

Siberian Huskies can detect movement at a greater distance than we can, but they can't see as well up close. They can also see better in less light, but can't distinguish many colors.

SOUND

Siberian Huskies, like all dogs, can hear about four times better than we can, and they can hear high pitched sounds especially well.

SMELL

The Husky's nose is his greatest sensory organ! A dog's sense of smell is so great he can follow a trail that's weeks old, detect odors diluted to one-millionth the concentration we'd need to notice them, even sniff out a person under water!

TOUCH

Siberian Huskies are social animals and love to be petted, groomed and played with.

TASTE

Siberian Huskies have fewer taste buds than we do, so they're likelier to try anything—and usually do, which is why it's important for their owners to monitor their food intake. Dogs are omnivorous, which means they eat meat as well as vegetables.

CHAPTER ONE

Getting to Know Your Siberian Husky

The lively, inquisitive, gregarious Siberian Husky is most content with an owner who is fascinated rather than exasperated by canine curiosity, who gladly returns a dog's affection and attention, who enjoys abundant amounts of routine physical activity and who is willing to understand and accept a dog for what that dog is meant to be.

MISCONCEPTIONS ABOUT THE HUSKY

The most common misconception about Siberian Huskies and, frankly, most of their Nordic cousins, is they have no sense and no intelligence. To label the breed so indicates that the speaker knows nothing about Siberians.

Look into the eyes of a Siberian Husky and you will discover the spirit of a self-sufficient, independent thinker.

2

Just what is canine intelligence? Is it a willingness to obey every human command without question? The Siberian doesn't think so, and he conveys his opinion on this most brazenly each day. No, to the Siberian and to those who love him, the intelligent dog is the one who decides for himself, according to his own thoughts at the moment, whether he will obey. In short, the Siberian may entertain a command, but he will obey only if he deems that to do so is relevant.

Such behavior is actually an ancient gift of survival to the human species, most clearly illustrated by the Siberian Husky's sled dog heritage. In both historic and current times, the Siberian has been entrusted with his musher's life. When that musher commands the lead dog to go right, but the dog knows through his superior canine senses that to go right means death, the dog follows his own instincts and disobeys. The savvy musher recognizes the dog's instincts and is grateful.

Of course, such a potentially headstrong dog is not what every dog owner looks for in a pet. Yet for those who do, there is nothing more stunning than the Siberian's mind at work—and nothing more challenging.

BORN TO RUN

Warning: NEVER allow your Siberian Husky to run loose!

In lists of instructions to new owners on the nuances of Siberian ownership, this statement is invariably the most important. Genetically programmed to run, your Siberian Husky will do so whenever he is offered the opportunity.

Siberians are obsessed with running. A hole in the fence, a slipped collar, a faint sound in a distant neighborhood, and your Siberian will answer that ancient genetic call within his soul and run, not because he is unhappy in his current surroundings, but because he simply must. He has no choice.

Though the running is genetic, nature has not provided the Siberian with an equally powerful homing instinct. The consequences, then, are clear. When your dog finally stops running, he will look around, probably not even realize he is lost and happily follow the first person he sees meandering by, even one who may mean harm.

NATURAL INCLINATIONS

Siberian Huskies love to chew (first while teething as puppies; later as a way of venting stress and excess energy), and they love to dig (a habit from their ancestors who

Prepare to meet the demands of the Siberian Husky before you bring one home. This responsible owner has cleared her schedule for lots of exercise, attention and training with her pets!

3

CHARACTERISTICS OF A SIBERIAN HUSKY

lively

curious

needs a lot of routine physical exercise

loves to run

independent-minded

devoted to family

4

would dig nests in the snow). Their need and desire to partake in these undeniably canine activities are directly related to the amount of attention and exercise they are receiving at a given time.

It's really not fair to bar your Siberian from digging and chewing entirely. Rather, it is best to accommodate your dog in a controlled manner that prevents wanton destruction of the house or yard. Doing this is simple enough: Provide your dog with plenty of sturdy chew toys to his liking (experimentation may be required to identify his favorites), and if possible, provide him with a digging place, a spot in the yard where he knows digging is allowed.

The digging place may be possible only if you have your own backyard, but there are alternatives. Winter offers ample digging opportunities if snow is on the ground, but in the summer, or in regions that get no snow, take your dog to the beach or perhaps to a river surrounded by soft earth. Here your dog can dig to his heart's content.

EXERCISE IS A MUST

The Siberian Husky, a veritable font of energy, requires plenty of exercise to help expend the energy he builds both in mind and body each day. This need not be a great deal of exercise—some fanciers suggest that a half hour a day of vigorous activity will suffice. Such a commitment will, for obvious reasons, benefit both dog and owner.

Running around in the yard alone day in and day out will not do. The Siberian's insatiable hunger for new sights and sounds must be satisfied as well as his physical needs. This is, after all, a world-class athlete bred for both endurance and adaptability to new environs.

Use your imagination in dealing with this dog. Refuse to do so and your Siberian surely will use his imagination, especially when it comes to dreaming up new and creative methods of destruction—all in the name of fun.

IN NEED OF A FAMILY

The Siberian Husky's life is family. The trouble is everyone is his family, a sentiment unappreciated by people who believe their Siberian will guard their home and hearth. Although Siberians are independent souls, their genetic code mandates an affinity for humans. They are profoundly devoted to their families—

and to virtually everyone else they happen to encounter.

While the Siberian's size, wolfy appearance and otherworldly eyes may be a deterrent to would-be attackers, this is no guard dog. Watchdog? Ask breeders. Sure, he'll watch anyone who comes into the home, and then show them where to find the valuables—all with that irrepressible Siberian smile.

AN ATTENTION-SEEKER

Siberians do not make good latchkey dogs. Their very social natures demand attention, and most will push their way into every family activity—and make everyone

5

This Siberian Husky demonstrates the speed and grace of the Nordic sled dog.

miserable if they can't do so. That desire has made the Siberian a very adaptable animal who loves to travel to new locales (with appropriate confinement and leash, of course), a longing that obviously stems from his historic travels on the ice.

Although the Siberian Husky revels in a frozen climate, he will adapt well to both rural and urban living in any region of the country. He simply asks for doses of companionship and exercise and that exercise sessions during the warmer months of the year be scheduled for the cooler hours of the day.

At the core of their adaptability is the Siberian's genuine love of family—and, especially, of children. Despite his independence, like all Nordic breeds, the Siberian Husky is uncannily attuned to family relationships. For obvious reasons, he is the ideal candidate for a multidog household and, in fact, may fare best in the company of other dogs. This in turn helps keep separation anxiety—and the resultant destructive behavior and neighbor-annoying howling—at bay.

TRAIN TO GAIN

Seeking professional help is a positive step toward teaching your Siberian what is expected of him

Proving that dogs aren't only man's best friend, this Siberian Husky gives some love to his friend, an English Cocker Spaniel.

Siberian Huskies and children are a perfect match!

and in forging the bond between the dog and his family. Obedience classes, for example, offer the ideal opportunity for both teaching and socializing dogs, and they prove invaluable in training owners as well. Be warned, however, that proper screening of potential trainers is imperative. Many professional dog trainers will readily confess that Nordic breeds can be a challenge to train—perhaps even a challenge that exceeds their own skills. But just as there are plenty of ideal Siberian Husky owners out there, so are there dog trainers who relish the opportunity to work with this breed.

The properly prepared owner and trainer understands that Siberians are quick learners, yet the dogs become easily and quickly bored, especially with training that involves endless repetition.

CHAPTER TWO

Homecoming

PICKING YOUR PUPPY

Choosing a puppy is usually a happy expedition to a breeder's home or kennel. Do not be put off if your puppy's owner puts you through the "third degree," asking questions like, "Where will the puppy sleep? Where will the puppy stay while you're at work? Do you have a fenced-in yard? If you owned a dog before, what happened to her?" All of these questions are designed to determine whether yours is a suitable home for the sweet puppy.

We shall assume you pass the "test" easily. Now, which puppy in the litter will be yours? The breeder may offer you a choice of only one or two. That's perfectly all right. There are very likely to be "reservations" for one or more of the babies—people who left deposits even before birth. Excellent breeders are sometimes booked well in advance of whelping.

If you do have a choice, be sure to pick a lively, alert animal, one who bounces up to greet you and wants to interact with the family. Do not be taken by the shy, shivering pup in the corner, no matter how "sorry" you may feel for her. Remember—she was raised under the same conditions as her littermates, and for reasons unknown to you, has not developed into a happy, well-adjusted animal. This could be temporary, due to a curable illness, or it could be genetic, meaning that she may grow to be an unhappy adult.

LAYING THE FOUNDATION

The first year that a dog or puppy spends with her new family is an adjustment period for all involved.

Regardless of your dog's age, when she arrives in the home the dynamics of the household are in for a change. Everyone will have to work to establish the new pet's place in the family and his or her own contribution to her care. This is also the ideal time to build a solid foundation that will carry the puppy or dog through her early months with her new family and into the years to come.

Puppies require a great deal of attention as you teach your puppy how to be a civilized canine citizen. In the weeks and months to come you and your puppy will need to address basic training (which may

9

Choosing a puppy is a well-thought-out process. This owner knows the Siberian Husky is a compatible breed to her lifestyle.

HOUSEHOLD DANGERS

Curious puppies and inquisitive dogs get into trouble not because they are bad, but simply because they want to investigate the world around them. It's our job to protect our dogs from harmful substances, like the following:

In the Garage

antifreeze

garden supplies, like snail and slug bait, pesticides, fertilizers, mouse and rat poisons

In the House

cleaners, especially pine oil

perfumes, colognes, aftershaves

medications, vitamins

office and craft supplies

electric cords

chicken or turkey bones

chocolate, onions

some house and garden plants, like ivy, oleander and poinsettia

begin with puppy kindergarten classes at 3 months of age); housetraining; canine manners at home and outside; and your puppy's overall health and physical development.

NATURAL CURIOSITY

The young Siberian Husky is more likely to be curious about than afraid of her surroundings. That curiosity could lead her to chew electrical cords, poisonous plants or glass Christmas ornaments (especially when teething begins at about 3 months of age). A selection of chew toys, constant supervision and puppy-proofing of the home environment (just as parents would do for a human child) could save your dog's life.

Curious or not, all puppies deserve some sensitivity from their owners to the great transition they are experiencing. In all your dealings with the young animal, you must make positive reinforcement the guiding concept and accept that your puppy will make mistakes and, of course, "have accidents" while she is working to understand what is expected of her.

It is also important to provide your puppy with a comforting, confined spot in the house that is all her own—perhaps a corner in the kitchen or in some other room of the house. Here your puppy can retreat to take a nap (puppies require a great deal of sleep), and here you may confine your puppy when she is left alone in the house.

Another option many breeders recommend is a crate—a denlike accommodation in which your puppy may be confined at night and when no one is at home. A crate provides your pet with both security and safety. One large enough for your puppy or dog to turn around in and furnished with a soft blanket and some chew toys may quickly become your puppy's, and someday your dog's, favorite voluntary sleeping place.

BASIC HEALTH CONCERNS

Within those first few months your puppy should receive a full series of vaccines, spaced several weeks apart, which culminate with the rabies vaccine at age 4 months. The immunity the vaccines provide is critical for a dog that will someday be spending a great deal of time outdoors and with other dogs. You should also have your puppy spayed or neutered. This ensures that a dog will never accidentally contribute to the problem of pet overpopulation. (See Chapter 3 for more information.)

SAFE HOUSING

All dogs need to chew; all dogs need protection from household dangers; all dogs need companionship; and all dogs, especially Siberian Huskies, need fail-safe confinement outdoors.

If your dog spends a great deal of time outdoors, an enclosed, chain-link dog kennel run, preferably the type with a roof, is ideal. A backyard with a fence that stands a minimum of 6 feet high is nice, too, but can prove dangerous, especially if the fencing is not anchored deeply into the ground or if your dog finds a small hole beneath the fence that

These curious Siberian Husky pups just can't help themselves when it comes to snooping around the house, so you must puppy-proof.

11

These two well-adjusted pals are neutered and vaccinated and enjoy optimum health and happiness because of it.

Providing your dog with a fenced-in yard will enable her to run and play without going astray.

she can excavate for freedom, adventure and running. Never underestimate a Siberian's digging abilities—or her skills as escape artist extraordinaire.

Siberians are not known as jumpers, but they have been known to scale or climb a fence, especially from the roof of a doghouse positioned next to that fence. And speaking of doghouses, the outdoor Siberian should have access to a well-insulated doghouse for shelter from the weather, but don't be surprised if she chooses not to use it in the snow. Many a Siberian prefers, like her ancestors, to curl up in a ball in the snow with her tail wrapped around her body in natural protection from the cold.

ACCESSORIES

The breeder should tell you what your puppy has been eating. Buy some of this food and have it on hand when your puppy arrives. Keep the puppy on the food and feeding schedule of the breeder, especially for the first few days. If you want to switch foods after that, introduce the new one slowly, gradually adding more and more to the old until it has been entirely replaced.

Your puppy will need a close-fitting nylon or cotton-webbed collar. This collar should be adjustable so that it can be used for the first couple of months. A puppy should never wear a choke chain or any other adult training collar.

In addition to a collar, you'll need a 4-to-6-foot-long leash. One made of nylon or cotton-webbed material is a fine and inexpensive first leash. It does not need to be more than half an inch in width. It is important to make sure that the clip is of excellent quality and cannot become unclasped on its own.

Excessive chewing can be partially resolved by providing a puppy with her own chew toys. Small-size dog biscuits are good for the teeth and also act as an amusing toy. Do not buy chew toys composed of compressed particles, as these particles disintegrate when chewed and can get stuck in the puppy's throat. Hard rubber toys are also good for chewing, as are large rawhide bones. Avoid the smaller chewsticks, as

IDENTIFY YOUR DOG

It is a terrible thing to think about, but your dog could somehow, someday, get lost or stolen. For safety's sake, every dog should wear a buckle collar with an identification tag. A tag is the first thing a stranger will look for on a lost dog. Inscribe the tag with your dog's name and your name and phone number.

There are two ways to permanently identify your dog. The first is a tattoo, placed on the inside of your dog's thigh. The tattoo should be your social security number or your dog's AKC registration number. The second is a microchip, a rice-sized pellet that is inserted under the dog's skin at the base of the neck, between the shoulder blades. When a scanner is passed over the dog, it will beep, notifying the person that the dog has a chip. The scanner will then show a code, identifying the dog.

13

A properly fitting collar is tight enough that it will not slip over the head, yet an adult's fingers fit comfortably under it.

These little chew toys go a long way! They protect your belongings from a teething puppy as well as provide your pet with hours of entertainment.

14

Puppyhood can be a trying time, but with proper training and lots of patience, you will both learn and grow.

they can splinter and choke the puppy. Anything given to a dog must be large enough that it cannot be swallowed.

The final starter items a puppy will need are a water bowl and food dish. You can select a smaller food dish for your puppy and then get a bigger one when your dog matures. Bowls are available in plastic, stainless steel and even ceramic. Stainless steel is probably the best choice, as it is practically indestructible. Nonspill dishes are available for the dog that likes to play in her water.

CHAPTER THREE

To Good Health

For thousands of years, the Siberian Husky had to be healthy—period. It was a matter of life and death, a matter of survival of the fittest.

GENERAL HEALTH CONCERNS

Aside from genetic conditions, the Siberian is just as prone to the more typical canine health problems as any other dog—even more prone, in fact, to such conditions as cut paws, leg injuries, embedded foxtails, poisoning and other conditions related to the Siberian's active out-door lifestyle. With this in mind, you must accept a great deal of responsibility in detecting potential problems as early as possible (the sooner treatment begins, the better the prognosis). You must then be

16

Thanks to their up-to-date vaccinations, these Siberian Husky pups (and their owners) can enjoy the outdoors with peace of mind.

urination); and limping are at the head of the list of symptoms that could indicate something as simple as an upset stomach or as serious as a failing internal organ. The better you, your dog's first line of defense, know your pet when he is healthy, the quicker you will recognize that something is wrong and seek treatment.

PREVENTIVE MEDICINE

Routine Care

Prevention is always the best medicine, and nowhere is this more evident than in the vision of the healthy dog. For obvious reasons, your veterinarian plays a key role here, thanks to his or her expertise in caring for patients who cannot communicate verbally about their health.

Your veterinarian is a valuable resource, but your part of the bargain is to bring your dog in at least once a year for a routine physical exam, booster vaccines, fecal exams and any other pertinent tests. Such a commitment makes life easier for both veterinarian and dog should a serious health condition be detected that will be more easily remedied with early treatment.

prepared to clearly communicate those findings to your veterinarian.

SIGNS OF SICKNESS

An unexplainable loss of appetite; diarrhea (especially diarrhea tinged with blood or mucus); abnormal discharges from the eyes, ears, nose or genital areas; depressed or listless behavior; lumps or bumps on the skin; poor coat quality; any unusual behavior changes; excessive thirst and urination (or strained

Vaccinations

A fundamental tenet of dog care is that dogs should be vaccinated every year. Nowhere is there a more eloquent method for fending off illness and saving hundreds of dollars in vet bills. Given that many people live with more than one Siberian Husky, current vaccines and the immunity they provide will help ensure that all within the household remain safe from communicable disease.

The dog's lifetime of vaccinations should begin during puppyhood. In his first weeks of life, the nursing puppy is protected by his mother's antibodies, but between 6 to 8 weeks of age, he must begin to develop his own immunity. This is facilitated by vaccines for canine distemper, hepatitis, leptospirosis, parainfluenza, parvovirus and coronavirus, all administered within a single DHLPPC vaccine. This vaccine must be repeated every few weeks for the next few months to help ensure effectiveness after the maternal antibodies within the puppy's system begin to subside.

Those maternal antibodies can present a serious problem, for though they protect a young puppy,

YOUR PUPPY'S VACCINES

Vaccines are given to prevent your dog from getting infectious diseases like canine distemper or rabies. Vaccines are the ultimate preventive medicine: They're given before your dog ever gets the disease so as to protect him from the disease. That's why it is necessary for your dog to be vaccinated routinely. Puppy vaccines start at 8 weeks of age for the five-in-one DHLPP vaccine and are given every three to four weeks until the puppy is 16 months old. Your veterinarian will put your puppy on a proper schedule and will remind you when to bring in your dog for shots.

17

This owner makes it her business to observe any changes in her dog's behavior.

they work to render vaccines useless, and thus void any vaccine immunity the puppy may be developing. A conservative vaccination

ADVANTAGES OF SPAY/NEUTER

The greatest advantage of spaying (for females) or neutering (for males) your dog is that you are guaranteed your dog will not produce puppies. There are too many puppies already available for too few homes. There are other advantages as well.

Advantages of Spaying

No messy heats.

No "suitors" howling at your windows or waiting in your yard.

No risk of pyometra (disease of the uterus) and decreased incidences of mammary cancer.

Advantages of Neutering

Decreased incidences of fighting, but does not affect the dog's personality.

Decreased roaming in search of bitches in season.

Decreased incidences of many urogenital diseases.

schedule therefore begins with the first vaccine at age 6 to 8 weeks, followed by three more vaccines spaced about three weeks apart until the puppy reaches 4 months of age (the coronavirus vaccine may require only a series of two vaccines).

Veterinarians' opinions on vaccine scheduling vary widely, and research into the subject is ongoing. Regardless of the original vaccine schedule you choose, your puppy should receive a DHLPPC booster at age 1, setting an annual pattern to be followed for the rest of his life. Another pattern is set by the all-important rabies vaccine, without which most communities will not allow a dog to be licensed. At 4 months, your puppy should be vaccinated against rabies, boosters for which must follow every year or every three years thereafter, depending on the particular vaccine.

Optional vaccines include those for Lyme disease and bordatella, or kennel cough (for dogs that are boarded at boarding kennels or frequently come into close contact with other dogs, particularly at dog shows).

COMMON DISEASES

Parvovirus

Canine parvovirus is a highly contagious and devastating illness. The hardy virus is usually transmitted through contaminated feces, but it can be carried on an infected dog's feet or skin. It strikes dogs of all ages and is most serious in young puppies.

Veterinarians can treat dogs with parvovirus, but the outcome varies. It depends on the age of the animal and severity of the disease. Treatment may include fluid therapy, medication to stop the severe diarrhea and antibiotics to prevent or stop secondary infection.

Young puppies receive some antibody protection against the disease from their mother, but they lose it quickly and must be vaccinated to prevent the disease. In most cases, vaccinated puppies are protected against the disease.

Coronavirus

Canine coronavirus is especially devastating to young puppies, causing depression, lack of appetite, vomiting that may contain blood and characteristically yellow-orange diarrhea. The virus is transmitted through feces, urine and saliva, and the onset of symptoms is usually rapid.

Dogs suffering from coronavirus are treated similarly to those suffering from parvovirus: fluid therapy, medication to stop diarrhea and vomiting and antibiotics if necessary.

Vaccinations are available to protect puppies and dogs against the virus and are recommended especially for those dogs in frequent contact with other dogs.

Distemper

Caused by a virus, the highly contagious distemper used to be the leading cause of infectious disease in

While a fence will help shield your Siberian Husky from harm, make sure it is high enough so he can't climb it. This fence is no match for this very eager Husky!

dogs. It is most common in unvaccinated puppies aged 3 to 8 months, but older dogs are susceptible as well. Because of vaccination programs, this is very rare nowadays.

Hepatitis

Infectious canine hepatitis can affect dogs of every age, but it is most severe in puppies. It primarily affects the dog's liver, kidneys and lining of the blood vessels. Highly contagious, it is transmitted through urine, feces and saliva.

Infectious canine hepatitis must be diagnosed and confirmed with a blood test. Ill dogs require hospitalization. Hepatitis is preventable in dogs by keeping vaccinations current.

PESTS AND PARASITES

Fleas

The most frustrating and the most irritating (if not the most dangerous) of all parasites to plague the dog and, subsequently, his owner is the flea. The signs are obvious: incessant scratching and the appearance of fleas and flea "dirt" (flea excrement) on your dog's skin. In some warmer areas fleas are a scourge year-round; in others, dogs are blessed with a respite during the colder seasons, but whenever fleas are about, the battle plan is the same.

To combat fleas effectively, regularly treat your dog (with flea shampoos, dips or sprays), his environment (the house, the dog's bedding, the owner's bedding—preferably with products that kill preadult as well as adult fleas) and the yard. Only in this way can you hope to destroy invading fleas at all life stages, in all their favored nesting spots. Remember, however, that the products you use to combat fleas are serious insecticides. To prevent toxic reactions in your dog, choose products that are compatible with one another and with your dog, and use them only as directed.

Ticks

Take your Siberian Husky out among the trees and vegetation, and he may just bring a tick or two home, stuck to his skin, gorging itself on his blood. Although basically harmless, ticks transmit Lyme disease and can be difficult to find on your dog's skin.

Through the years many tales have circulated on how to remove ticks. The true remedy is simple: Just pull it out. On finding a tick on your dog, douse it with alcohol, then grasp its bulbous body firmly with tweezers and pull out straight, smoothly and firmly. (If tweezers are not available, use fingertips, preferably protected by a glove, a piece of plastic wrap or even a piece of paper or tissue.)

Dogs that frequently cavort in tick country, as Siberians certainly do, should be sprayed before doing so with a flea and tick spray. Your dog should then be examined carefully from head to tail at the conclusion of every romp.

LYME DISEASE—Should you locate and remove a tick, watch for arthritis-like signs or any other potential signs of illness for the next few weeks. These can be signals of Lyme disease, caused by a bacteria that, if diagnosed early, can be treated effectively and relatively simply with antibiotics.

Heartworm Disease

This parasite is extremely dangerous. Transmitted by infected

FLEAS AND TICKS

There are so many safe, effective products available now to combat fleas and ticks that—thankfully—they are less of a problem. Prevention is key, however. Ask your veterinarian about starting your puppy on a flea/tick repellent right away. With this, regular grooming and environmental controls, your dog and your home should stay pest-free. Without this attention, you risk infesting your dog and your home, and you're in for an ugly and costly battle to clear up the problem.

mosquitoes, the preadult heartworm makes its way through your dog's bloodstream to his heart, where it grows into adulthood and works to carry on the life cycle of its species. If left untreated, heartworm will cause signs of coughing and lethargy in its victim, whom it will ultimately kill.

Treatment of heartworm disease is itself toxic, traumatic and complicated, but prevention is simple. First, an annual blood test will determine whether or not your dog has been infected. The test is then followed by the administration of effective, reasonably priced daily or monthly preventives that will help ensure your heartworm-free dog

PREVENTIVE CARE PAYS

Using common sense, paying attention to your dog and working with your veterinarian, you can minimize health risks and problems. Use vet-recommended flea, tick and heartworm preventive medications; feed a nutritious diet appropriate for your dog's size, age and activity level; give your dog sufficient exercise and regular grooming; train and socialize your dog; keep current on your dog's shots; and enjoy all the years you have with your friend.

remains that way. Although heartworm is not a major problem in all regions of the nation, it has affected dogs from coast to coast, and the wise owner takes the precaution, knowing how devastating the alternative can be.

Internal Parasites

Few dogs of any breed make it through a long, healthy life without experiencing an infestation of internal parasites. Roundworms, hookworms, tapeworms (transmitted by fleas), whipworms and others thrive in the innards of a dog. While such an infestation can be dangerous to young puppies, worms rarely present grave danger to adult dogs. They

should, nevertheless, be eradicated swiftly.

TAPEWORMS
Tapeworms also attach to the intestinal wall to absorb nutrients. As they grow they form new segments; these segments, which look like grains of rice, can be found in the dog's stools or on the area around the dog's anus if the dog is infected. The best way to prevent a tapeworm infestation is with a good flea control program, since tapeworms are acquired when a dog chews a flea bite and swallows a flea.

ROUNDWORMS
Roundworms occasionally infest adult dogs and people, and often infest puppies. Roundworms are transmitted via feces, when an animal walks in or eats infested feces—a good reason to pick up your dog's droppings daily and prevent your dog from investigating other dogs' feces.

If treated early, roundworms are not serious. But they must be detected and treated. Puppies with roundworms will not thrive and will appear thin but pot-bellied, with a dull coat.

HOOKWORMS

Hookworms (so called because of the hooklike teeth by which they attach themselves) live in the small intestines of dogs and suck blood from the intestinal wall. When they detach and move to a new location, the old wound continues to bleed because of the anticoagulant the worm injects when it bites. Consequently, bloody diarrhea is usually the first sign of a problem.

Like roundworms, hookworm eggs are transmitted through feces or, if conditions are right, they hatch in the soil. They then attach themselves to the feet of their new hosts, where they can burrow into the skin and migrate to the intestinal tract.

WHIPWORMS

Adult whipworms live in the large intestine, where they feed on blood. The eggs are passed in the dog's stool and can live in the soil for many years. A heavily infested dog will have diarrhea that's often watery or bloody. The dog may appear thin and anemic, with a poor coat. Whipworms can be difficult to detect, as the worms do not continually shed eggs. Therefore, a stool sample may be clear one day and show eggs the next.

The best ways to combat this unpleasant problem are to prevent your dog from running free and thus be exposed to various sources of worm transmission (feces of other

23

Being one of the most active and curious outdoor dogs, the Siberian Husky more frequently comes in contact with parasites, insect bites and poisonous plants.

WHAT'S WRONG WITH MY DOG?

We've listed some common symptoms of health problems and their possible causes. If any of the following symptoms appear serious or persist for more than 24 hours, make an appointment to see your veterinarian immediately.

CONDITIONS	POSSIBLE CAUSES
DIARRHEA	Intestinal upset, typically caused by eating something bad or over-eating. Can also be a viral infection, a bad case of nerves or anxiety or a parasite infection. If you see blood in the feces, get to the vet right away.
VOMITING/RETCHING	Dogs regurgitate fairly regularly (bitches for their young), whenever something upsets their stomachs, or even out of excitement or anxiety. Often dogs eat grass, which, because it's indigestible in its pure form, irritates their stomachs and causes them to vomit. Getting a good look at *what* your dog vomited can better indicate what's causing it.
COUGHING	Obstruction in the throat; virus (kennel cough); roundworm infestation; congestive heart failure.
RUNNY NOSE	Because dogs don't catch colds like people, a runny nose is a sign of congestion or irritation.
LOSS OF APPETITE	Because most dogs are hearty and regular eaters, a loss of appetite can be your first and most accurate sign of a serious problem.
LOSS OF ENERGY (LETHARGY)	Any number of things could be slowing down your dog, from an infection to internal tumors to overexercise—even overeating.

dogs, tapeworm-carrying fleas, etc.) and to examine your dog's feces for signs of infestation. Even without signs of infestation, bring a fecal sample to your veterinarian once or twice a year for examination. If worms or their eggs are present, your veterinarian can prescribe the appropriate dewormer for that particular strain.

CONDITIONS	POSSIBLE CAUSES
STINKY BREATH	Imagine if you never brushed your teeth! Foul-smelling breath indicates plaque and tartar buildup that could possibly have caused infection. Start brushing your dog's teeth.
LIMPING	This could be caused by something as simple as a hurt or bruised pad, to something as complicated as hip dysplasia, torn ligaments or broken bones.
CONSTANT ITCHING	Probably due to fleas, mites or an allergic reaction to food or environment (your vet will need to help you determine what your dog's allergic to).
RED, INFLAMED, ITCHY SPOTS	Often referred to as "hot spots," these are particularly common on coated breeds. They're caused by a bacterial infection that gets aggravated as the dog licks and bites at the spot.
BALD SPOTS	These are the result of excessive itching or biting at the skin so that the hair follicles are damaged; excessively dry skin; mange; calluses; and even infections. You need to determine what the underlying cause is.
STINKY EARS/HEAD SHAKING	Take a look under your dog's ear flap. Do you see brown, waxy build-up? Clean the ears with something soft and a special cleaner, and don't use cotton swabs or go too deep into the ear canal.
UNUSUAL LUMPS	Could be fatty tissue, could be something serious (infection, trauma, tumor). Don't wait to find out.

Giardiasis

Few can resist the allure of a cool mountain stream in the midst of a long hike in the mountains. But within that stream or any other natural body of water may lurk the protozoan that causes giardiasis.

The active Siberian Husky (or its active owner) may happily lap up the nectar from this lovely stream, only later to be plagued by persistent diarrhea (a sign that requires immediate veterinary attention no matter what is causing it). Some affected dogs exhibit no signs, but either way, this is a highly contagious parasitic condition that may also be transmitted through the feces of an infected dog.

Although giardiasis can be treated successfully with medication, prevention is preferable, pursued by keeping your dog's housing, feed dishes and toys sanitized; by preventing your dog from touching feces from other dogs that may be infected; and by bringing along an ample supply of your dog's own water to keep him hydrated on the trail, no matter how inviting that mountain stream might be.

THE EYES

CATARACTS—This condition of the lens usually appears as a milky whitish or bluish cloudiness beneath the surface of the eye. While "senile" cataracts are common in older dogs as a natural part of aging, as are cataracts in diabetic dogs, hereditary cataracts, often called juvenile cataracts, which affect younger dogs

(usually before the age of 5), are all too common in Siberian Huskies. Some cataracts may not substantially interfere with the dog's quality of life, but if the condition severely impairs the dog's vision, the cataracts may be removed surgically.

As with progressive retinal atrophy, another genetic eye condition common to Siberians, dogs with hereditary cataracts or from lines in which the condition appears should not be bred.

CONJUNCTIVITIS—Although a slight eye discharge may be normal in the healthy Siberian Husky, a profuse, often discolored discharge, red, swollen eyelid tissues and itchiness are the classic signs of conjunctivitis, an often contagious inflammation of the lining of the eyelids. Conjunctivitis is usually caused by an allergic reaction to pollens, a bacterial infection, a structural defect in the eyelids or other illnesses (as a secondary infection).

Dogs that actively participate in outdoor activities, a group from which the Siberian Husky proudly hails, can also develop conjunctivitis from foreign objects such as seeds and other plant materials that become embedded in the eye.

These baby blues are this Siberian Husky's most striking feature.

Conjunctivitis, though rarely serious and fairly easy to treat, can be very irritating to your dog and should receive veterinary attention.

PROGRESSIVE RETINAL ATROPHY—This is a condition in which, at 5 to 7 years of age, the cells in the retina at the back of the dog's eye begin to degenerate. You will probably first notice signs of night blindness in your dog, which gradually leads to a complete loss of his sight. Prevention is the only "treatment." Because it is a hereditary disease, only Huskies that are certified free of eye problems by the Canine Eye Registration Foundation (CERF) should be chosen to carry on their lines.

THE HIPS

HIP DYSPLASIA—Hip dysplasia is an abnormality in the structure of the hip joint that strikes fear in the hearts of dog owners who suddenly notice their dogs beginning to go lame in the hind legs.

While virtually no dog is immune, the Siberian Husky is not generally prone to the disease, yet ethical breeders breed only dogs certified clear by the Orthopedic Foundation for Animals (OFA).

THE URINARY TRACT

Cystitis

Also known as a bladder infection, cystitis occurs when bacteria infect and inflame the bladder. The affected dog will stop to urinate more frequently than usual, strain to urinate without much success and perhaps break his housetraining. Also, his urine may show blood.

Any sign of urinary tract problems should be directed as soon as possible to your veterinarian, who will diagnose the condition with a urine sample. If cystitis is diagnosed, your veterinarian will prescribe antibiotics for your dog and probably ask that he be brought back in several weeks for a follow-up urinalysis to ensure the infection has been vanquished.

To help prevent cystitis, your dog should get plenty of exercise and thus ample opportunity to urinate (no drastic lifestyle change for the Siberian Husky) and drink plenty of water throughout the day to flush the bladder routinely. If this or any other urinary ailment is left untreated, it may lead to more serious problems, in this case damage to the kidneys, not to mention the discomfort it causes your dog.

Kidney Failure

The healthy kidneys clean wastes from the blood and rid the body of those wastes quickly and efficiently. If the kidneys fail, the wastes and their toxins remain in the body, and a general breakdown of organs occurs, eventually claiming the life of your dog. Various causes can lead to the development of acute or chronic kidney failure, either of which requires immediate medical attention.

To protect those canine kidneys, you should offer your dog plenty of opportunities to urinate throughout the day, which will ease the stress on these vital organs. Your dog should be forbidden from running loose, a habit that could lead him to encounters with substances toxic to the kidneys, such as sweet-tasting antifreeze.

Stones

In dogs, urinary stones are far more likely to form in the bladder than in the kidneys. They may form as large, often rounded, single stones or small, rough, gravel-like stones, either of which can be extremely painful to your dog. They are dangerous because they block urine flow. Veterinary intervention is critical for both the health and comfort of your dog. Stones can be treated through diet, medication and, in severe cases, surgery.

THE SKIN

Allergies

Your dog's skin is prone to a number of allergies, some extremely difficult to control. Although some dogs, like some humans, are allergic to pollens, grasses and food ingredients, flea saliva is a very common allergy, which can continue long after the fleas have been obliterated from both your dog and his environment.

An allergic dog will typically scratch and bite at the offending area of his body, perhaps endlessly licking his itchy feet after romping through a field of allergy-inducing grass.

Allergies may be relieved with oral, topical or injected medications prescribed by your veterinarian as well as by attempts to limit your dog's access to his allergens (some,

29

thankfully, are seasonal). Commitment to a flea control program also reaps obvious benefits.

Hot Spots

Hot spots—nickel-sized, red, sore and oozy patches on your dog's skin—can seem to develop overnight from no particular cause. They are deep skin infections, often caused by an insect bite or other irritation that develops into an itchy spot that the dog then licks at until it's red and raw. Your veterinarian should examine the spot to make sure it's not caused by fleas, mange

This Siberian Husky's beautiful coat and glimmering eyes indicate that he is in perfect health.

or an allergy. He or she will also give you an antibiotic or topical anti-inflammatory medicine to treat the spot.

Mites

These tiny parasites that thrive within the skin of your dog can cause two serious conditions that can prove difficult and time-consuming to treat: sarcoptic mange and demodectic mange.

Mites operate by burrowing into the skin, causing severe inflammation and hair loss. You may believe your dog is suffering from a generalized skin allergy only to be informed by your veterinarian after he or she examines a skin scraping of the affected area that mites are the true cause of your dog's condition. This news is never good.

An infestation of mites and the endless irritation and high contagion it brings can drive both you and your dog crazy. Your dog cannot rid himself of the discomfort, and you are faced with a rigorous treatment regimen. This may include the repeated application of medicated shampoos, dips and parasiticidal agents for weeks, antibiotics for secondary infections and vigorous

treatment of the environment until the mites are gone.

Tumors

Siberians usually are not prone to skin tumors, but you should still watch carefully for them, ideally during routine grooming sessions.

GASTROINTESTINAL ILLNESS

Canine Bloat

Canine bloat is an intensely painful, life-threatening condition in which gas, air and fluid build up in the dog's stomach, causing it subsequently to bloat and ultimately to twist. This acute trauma hits suddenly and violently. As it progresses, the internal turmoil squeezes the veins and arteries that transport the body's blood supply and impairs the dog's ability to breathe. Soon after, the dog will die.

Bloat is a condition that requires immediate emergency veterinary attention. Your veterinarian, by inserting a stomach tube through your dog's nose, may be able to release the gas buildup in the stomach. If at this point the stomach has twisted, no such release is possible, and surgery to untwist and anchor the stomach is the only option. To further complicate matters, the prognosis is always uncertain.

The good news is that because bloat is most common in large, deep-chested dogs, the Siberian is neither a natural nor common candidate for the condition. The bad news is that despite breed predispositions or lack thereof, bloat can happen to any dog at any time. Basic prevention, then, is imperative and not all that cumbersome.

To help prevent the conditions that can lead to bloat, feed your dog in several smaller meals a day rather than one large meal. Also schedule meals for the same times each day, do not allow your dog to exercise after a large meal, try to prevent your dog from gulping down his food (a frequent phenomenon if your dog perceives competition for his dinner from other dogs), and watch your dog carefully after he eats, so you can act quickly if you notice signs of bloat (profuse saliva-tion, a distending abdomen, restless-ness, general discomfort and unsuc-cessful attempts to vomit or defecate).

OUTDOOR EMERGENCIES

Although it is not fair to prevent your dog from participating in the activities he loves best nor to pre-vent accidents entirely, it is possible and even imperative to prepare for their occurrence and know how to handle them.

Physical preparation for emer-gencies means assembling a first-aid kit. So armed, you must further pre-pare by learning and understanding what dangers might lurk out there in the great outdoors and by know-ing how to act if called on to do so.

Bleeding Wounds

In the event of an injury that causes bleeding, a safe and effective way to

Be prepared! It is not unusual for an active Siberian Husky, the quintessen-tial outdoor dog, to fall victim to outdoor emergencies.

31

WHEN TO CALL THE VETERINARIAN

In any emergency situation, you should call your veterinarian immediately. Try to stay calm when you call, and give the vet or the assistant as much information as possible before you leave for the clinic. That way, the staff will be able to take immediate, specific action when you arrive. Emergencies include:

- Bleeding or deep wounds
- Hyperthermia (overheating)
- Shock
- Dehydration
- Abdominal pain
- Burns
- Fits
- Unconsciousness
- Broken bones
- Paralysis

Call your veterinarian if you suspect any health troubles.

stop the flow of blood is to cover the wound with clean gauze from the first-aid kit or any available clean cloth and to apply direct pressure to the source of the wound. Other

methods exist, such as arterial pressure and applying a tourniquet, but these require more extensive training. Obviously then, it's best to obtain such training long before ever needing to apply the skills.

As is done in the care of wounds in humans, no matter how minor, a dog's wound should first be cleaned thoroughly to prevent infection (this may require cutting away some of the hair to gain access to the wound). Next, treat the wound with antibiotic ointment, and then dress it with clean bandage materials.

Severe injuries such as puncture wounds, bites from other animals and wounds that require stitches must be treated by your veterinarian as soon as possible.

Shock

Anytime a dog (or a human being) suffers a severe injury or illness that affects his blood flow and thus the heart's function, that dog is in danger of going into shock. Usually the result of severe bleeding, but also possible from acute illness, shock results from an inadequate flow of blood.

The most common cause of shock in dogs, one all too familiar to the Siberian Husky allowed to run loose, is a confrontation with a moving car. In the face of massive blood loss, the heart does all it can to get blood to the dog's vital organs, which cannot function without blood and consequently shut down. In time, if the situation is not reversed, the dog will die.

A dog in shock will experience a dramatic drop in body temperature and correspondingly cold extremities. He will seem dazed and disoriented and breathe rapidly. His pulse will feel fast yet weak, and his mucous membranes will pale. Your dog may be frightened, but muzzling must be done only as a last resort because it can impair your dog's already panicked attempts to breathe.

Depending on the particular case, full treatment requires not only tending to the underlying cause of shock, but also stabilizing the resulting chaos in the internal organs. In most cases, this is a job for experts.

Until you can get your dog to your veterinarian, cover him with a blanket or a jacket to help his body maintain a normal temperature; try to stop any severe bleeding; prevent him from eating or drinking; and keep him comfortable, quiet and

POISON ALERT

If your dog has ingested a potentially poisonous substance, waste no time. Call the National Animal Poison Control Center hot line:

(800) 548-2423 ($30 per case) or

(900) 680-0000 ($20 first five minutes; $2.95 each additional minute)

calm (a calm owner is equally helpful). Such measures can save your dog's life in that critical time before he receives emergency veterinary treatment.

Your dog should be moved only as necessary: Movement may cause further injury and complicate his condition. A shock victim may fare best lying down, from which he can be moved with a large blanket or sheet folded into a hammock-style stretcher. If no such items or other hands are available for carrying your dog this way, you may have to carry him in your arms.

Poisoning

Poisoning can occur from a variety of sources, anything from a pool of enticing, sweet-tasting antifreeze left in the driveway to poisonous plants

33

your dog finds both inside and out, to cleaning solutions left in an open cabinet.

Heatstroke

Siberian Huskies are adaptable creatures, but they, like all dogs, will easily succumb to overheating—which can occur unbelievably quickly. The affected dog will pant rapidly, his mucous membranes will appear bright red, he will be unsteady and he possibly will vomit. Because your dog's system cannot cool itself, heatstroke is an unconditional, life-threatening emergency.

To help cool down the overheated dog, get him quickly to a cool environment (ideally an air-conditioned room, but in a pinch some shade on the trail will suffice). Try to cool his body with cool (not cold) water. The dog's average normal rectal temperature of 101.3°F can soar as high as 106°F with heatstroke. To take your dog's temperature, clean the rectal thermometer with alcohol, coat it with petroleum jelly, hold up his tail and gently insert the bulbous end of the thermometer into the anal canal.

Protecting your dog from this life-threatening trauma is simple enough: Schedule exercise sessions during the cooler times of the day; never leave your dog in the car in temperatures that are even moderately warm (the interior temperature will soar dramatically in minutes, even with the window open); make sure your dog has constant access to plenty of shade and fresh, clean water.

SAYING GOOD-BYE

The time comes in every relationship with a dog when you must say good-bye. After a life of fine care and companionship, we inevitably outlive our dogs. Most who choose to live with dogs know the time must come to make some hard decisions.

While an older dog, even one whose lifestyle has changed dramatically with age, can live for years in comfort and contentment, he will inevitably reach the day when he can no longer sufficiently enjoy his life.

The decision for painless, peaceful euthanasia can be one of the most devastating a dog owner is ever asked to make. Once done, it may leave the individual with feelings of loneliness and guilt because dogs, especially dogs as gregarious and people-loving as the Siberian Husky, become important members of the family. But that decision is the only humane option when your dog is suffering badly. Such dear friends deserve compassion and courage from their owners at this critical juncture.

The grieving process is very real when your dog, a longtime family fixture, is no longer around. While outsiders may respond to the loss with such comments as "he was only a dog," you must try to ignore that and allow the grief to play out.

Because many Siberians live in multiple-dog households, the presence of the other dogs can be a comfort. But for the dog that presided over a one-dog domain, the only remedy for the owner he left behind may be in obtaining another dog, not as a replacement, but as a new family member.

Some seek a new canine addition to the family immediately; others must wait until they have completed the grieving process. When and how you obtain a new dog is a very personal decision, one best left not to well-meaning friends who try to surprise their sad friend with a puppy but to the prospective owner who should choose his or her own companion carefully and in his or her own time.

It is this owner and this dog, after all, who will be sharing the years ahead together in a very special relationship.

The Siberian Husky has enjoyed a very special relationship with humans for thousands of years, which will surely continue for thousands more.

CHAPTER FOUR

Positively Nutritious

For such an active dog, on the trail or in the home, only a high-quality, balanced diet can properly fuel that legendary font of energy that lies within, keeping her body healthy and her mind alert. To live up to her birthright as an energetic, fun-loving dog, an owner has no choice but to ensure that this breathtakingly beautiful machine remains ready and able to keep up with any activity that strikes her fancy.

BASIC NUTRITION

All dogs require a balanced diet. According to the principles of basic canine nutrition, the nutrients must all be present—proteins, fats, carbohydrates, vitamins and minerals—but they must blend within a balanced formula. This formula lies at the heart of that beautiful coat, those shining eyes and those efficient internal organs.

The Siberian Husky is the perfect combination of companion and athlete, thus requiring a diet worthy of both callings.

A common misconception is that if a little is good, more must be better—not so in nutrition, canine or otherwise. The nutrients seek balance and harmony with each other for the good of the body at large. Get too little or too much of one, especially vitamins and minerals, and the other nutrients, as well as the bodily functions with which they interact, can all be sent into a tailspin.

The moral of the story? Overnutrition can be just as dangerous as malnutrition. With one exception . . . water. This is the nutrient a dog can almost never have enough of. Like our bodies,

dogs' bodies are largely composed of water, and dehydration is a serious threat to life. Make sure your Husky always has access to a bowl of clean, cool, fresh water. Wash any water bowls thoroughly every day, especially outdoor bowls, to keep bacteria and flies at bay. The only time water should be restricted is just before bed during early puppyhood, when housetraining rules are being established.

FOOD QUALITY

The best diet for a dog, any dog, is simple: a high-quality commercial

FOOD ALLERGIES

If your puppy or dog seems to itch all the time for no apparent reason, she could be allergic to one or more ingredients in her food. This is not uncommon, and it's why many foods contain lamb and rice instead of beef, wheat or soy. Have your dog tested by your veterinarian, and be patient while you strive to identify and eliminate the allergens from your dog's food (or environment).

Stainless steel food and water bowls are the most sterile and the easiest to clean.

diet, readily available in pet supply and grocery stores. The key phrase is "high-quality." In other words, ignore the generics. Safest are those foods approved by the Association of American Feed Control Officials (noted on the packaging). This approval means the food meets the standards of what is currently accepted as best for man's best friend.

Such foods come in several forms. The simplest and most hassle-free is dry kibble, although some owners like to spice up the kibble with a touch of canned food thrown in for flavor (some owners feed half and half). With a quality product, as long as the correct amount and balance are there—and as long as the dog shines like a picture of health—all is well.

FIGHTING FAT

Excess poundage is not the sole domain of the older dog. Owners who revel in sharing a slice of birthday cake with the family pet or allowing her to "clear" the dinner plates every night must realize that obesity is a major health risk for dogs that undermines an animal's quality and length of life.

Fortunately, it is rare to see an obese Siberian Husky. Yet breeders warn that you must take great care not to overfeed this animal, which was bred for an efficient metabolism and limited dietary needs. That extraordinary Siberian metabolism may be overwhelmed by a modern diet, and the dog could gain weight on the amounts of food prescribed on the package for that size dog.

For that rogue Siberian Husky that has succumbed to the lure of too many table scraps from her master's table, light canine diets are available. These satisfy her hunger while remaining lower in fat and calories to facilitate weight loss—assuming, of course, that you also commit to reducing or, preferably, eliminating treats and table scraps from your dog's menu.

HOW MUCH TO FEED YOUR HUSKY

When you bring your Husky puppy home, if she's between 6 and 10 weeks old, you can expect to feed her three or four times a day. Start your puppy on kibble, preferably the same brand she was eating before you got her. If you want to switch brands, do so gradually, mixing small amounts of the new food in with the old until all the old is replaced with the new.

GROWTH STAGE FOODS

Once upon a time, there was puppy food and there was adult dog food. Now there are foods for puppies, young adults/active dogs, less active dogs and senior citizens. What's the difference between these foods? They vary by the amounts of nutrients they provide for the dog's growth stage/activity level.

Less active dogs don't need as much protein or fat as growing, active dogs; senior dogs don't need some of the nutrients vital to puppies. By feeding a high-quality food that's appropriate for your dog's age and activity level, you're benefiting your dog and yourself. Feed too much protein to a couch potato and she'll have energy to spare, which means a few more trips around the block will be needed to burn it off. Feed an adult diet to a puppy, and risk growth and development abnormalities that could affect her for a lifetime.

The person from whom you got your puppy can probably recommend how much to feed her at each meal, and you can ask your veterinarian when you take your pup in for her examination and vaccines. Mix the kibble with some warm water and let it soften some before feeding.

At around 12 weeks of age, you can cut back to three meals a day,

How to Read the Dog Food Label

With so many choices on the market, how can you be sure you are feeding the right food to your dog? The information is all there on the label—if you know what you're looking for.

Look for the nutritional claim right up top. Is the food "100 percent nutritionally complete"? If so, it's for nearly all life stages; "growth and maintenance," on the other hand, is for early development; puppy foods are marked as such, as are foods for senior dogs.

Ingredients are listed in descending order by weight. The first three or four ingredients will tell you the bulk of what the food contains. Look for the highest-quality ingredients, like meats and grains, to be among them.

The Guaranteed Analysis tells you what levels of protein, fat, fiber and moisture are in the food, in that order. While these numbers are meaningful, they won't tell you much about the quality of the food. Nutritional value is in the dry matter, not the moisture content.

In many ways, seeing is believing. If your dog has bright eyes, a shiny coat, a good appetite and a good energy level, chances are her diet's fine. Your dog's breeder and your veterinarian are good sources of advice if you're still confused.

reducing to two when your pup's 6 months or older.

There is no set serving amount ideal for every Siberian. For the adult, depending on your individual dog and her calling, she may require anywhere from 2 to 4 cups of dry food a day. Your veterinarian can help determine the ideal amount for your dog, assisted, of course, by your knowledge of your pet.

Keep Track of What You Feed

Feeding methods are also something to think about. Some dogs can be free-fed, meaning dry food may be left for them at all times, allowing them to nibble whenever they feel a pang. This is not a recommended feeding style, however, for several reasons. First is health. One of the earliest signs that your dog may not be feeling well is a loss of appetite. A healthy Husky should be eager for mealtime. If you free-feed your dog and she doesn't go for the food right away, you may not suspect her appetite is off until the end of the day when you see no food was eaten. Another reason not to free-feed has to do with behavior. As the meal provider for your dog, you gain elevated status and control. Free-feed, and your dog doesn't need you to have her appetite sated.

Along these lines, you shouldn't even be too generous with scheduled mealtimes. If your dog doesn't finish her food within fifteen minutes of putting the bowl down, pick the bowl up and don't feed her again until the next mealtime. Healthy Huskies have healthy appetites and should have no problem finishing meals.

Dogs may also exhibit preferences for certain foods. That's fine, but once one works, stick with it. Variety need not be an issue.

It is always a pleasure to give the Siberian Husky a well-deserved treat!

41

A well-fed Husky is a happy Husky.

CHAPTER FIVE

Putting on the Dog

One fact Siberian Husky owners must face very early in their relationship with this dog is that when walking down the street with a Siberian in tow, it's the dog that will receive most of the attention from onlookers. This attention should cause no animosity nor come as a surprise because the dog's great beauty is why most people find themselves attracted to this breed in the first place.

A DOUBLE-COATED DOG

The Siberian's double coat—the soft, dense, fluffy undercoat protected by longer guard hairs—works to warm the dog in the sub-zero temperatures from which the breed hails. As an added benefit, the body's own self-maintenance of this coat is as inspiring as the efficiency with which the coat functions.

While the Siberian sheds as any other dog of its coat length does, once or twice a year most experience an unusually heavy shed, referred to as "blowing coat." Over several weeks, the undercoat comes out in great, soft handfuls. The prepared caretaker in turn stands ready with comb and brush to keep the process under control.

Despite how lovely the Siberian may look in full coat, when it comes time to blow, you must resist the impulse to brush your dog only superficially, bypassing the skin and therefore retaining the appearance of a full coat. Without proper groom-ing (more like harvesting) during this time, those loose hairs will become trapped next to the skin, retaining moisture and heat that can lead to skin problems, especially in warmer temperatures.

This is not to suggest that in the summer's heat, the Siberian Husky should be shaved. On the contrary, your dog's unique coat works just as effectively to keep him cool as it does to keep him warm; to remove that natural protection by shaving is to expose the skin to elements it was never meant to see.

To maintain the beauty of the Siberian Husky, a surprisingly minimal amount of effort is required.

GROOMING TOOLS

pin brush	scissors
slicker brush	nail clippers
flea comb	tooth-cleaning equipment
towel	shampoo
mat rake	conditioner
grooming glove	clippers

ROUTINE BRUSHING

Short yet thorough brushing sessions several times a week will prevent a monumental job later when the coat begins to blow, and it will keep shedding under control in the meantime. Brushing distributes the natural oils of the skin and coat to keep both healthy and lovely to look at, and to dogs who have been trained to sit and relax for grooming (preferably at a young age), it feels good, too.

The Siberian, like most of the Nordic breeds, doesn't usually carry the traditional doggy odor common to the species. All in all, the Siberian is a very clean breed. Routine brushing helps maintain that cleanliness by removing the dirt, plant materials and even bugs that hitch a ride in a Siberian's coat during a normal, active day. Such sessions also offer you a chance to examine your dog for lumps or bumps on the skin or anything unusual that may signal a developing health problem.

GROOMING TOOLS

Which tools you decide on is really based on what you are most comfortable using. It is on your shoulders, after all, that the grooming responsibility falls. The only rule is that your dog be brushed or combed down to the skin. There's no point and no benefit to doing a superficial job.

The comb or brush should glide easily through the Siberian's coat, for this is a breed not generally prone to matting. Mats can develop from the soft hair at the base of the ears, in the armpit or on the groin, yet routine grooming should help prevent this. Should mats develop, however, they must be removed to prevent skin rashes or infections (working them out or attempting detangling can be extremely painful to your dog). Loose mats that are far enough away from the skin can be cut out with blunt-tipped scissors; those close to the skin are best removed by a professional groomer with clippers to prevent injury.

BATHING YOUR HUSKY

Bathing may be done by turning your dog over to a capable groomer, or you can do it at home. Should you choose the latter approach, the following steps offer some basic guidelines.

First, gather the supplies. In addition to several clean towels and perhaps a washcloth and plastic rinsing cup, you will need appropriate shampoo. This should be one formulated specifically for dogs (or for puppies if your dog is a youngster).

Some pet owners bathe their dogs in the bathtub, whereas others prefer using a garden hose outdoors on hot summer days (with a properly restrained dog). A clean plastic garbage can or ice tub filled with water can also act as effective outdoor bathtubs. Regardless of the bathtub style used, lukewarm water reaps the greatest results and elicits the least resistance from the dog.

The actual bathing process begins with a thorough brushing to remove loose hairs that may mat up once the coat is wet. At this point, some groomers place cotton in the ears and mineral oil in the eyes for protection. If you don't wish to do this, you must take great care to keep water out of the ears and soap out of the eyes.

Next, wet the coat. It may prove difficult to saturate, but keep at it. The coat must be wet to the skin, after which it's time to apply the shampoo. Scrub your dog gently from head to toe (leaving the head and face for last often makes the ordeal more bearable for some

This Siberian Husky shows his appreciation to his owner, who takes great care of her pet's coat.

45

dogs). Work the shampoo down to the skin and into every nook and cranny, from between the toes to the genital and anal areas.

Once you are convinced your dog has been thoroughly cleansed, begin rinsing. Rinse and rinse and rinse, and when it appears that no more suds or bubbles are falling from the body, rinse again. Shampoo left on the coat or skin can dry out both and cause itching. With a coat as thick as the Siberian's, the rinsing process can at times seem endless.

Because the Siberian Husky is naturally a clean breed, your dog will rarely need bathing. A few times a year should suffice.

DRY THOROUGHLY

Once the coat is clean, drying begins. After an initial towel drying, try blow-drying the coat for a few minutes (on warm, not hot). After that, air-drying can finish the job. The key here is to keep your dog indoors or similarly sheltered where he will not be exposed to cold or wind until he is completely dry, undercoat and outercoat. Reaching that point can literally take all day.

When his coat is dry or almost so, brush him again. This will remove those hairs inevitably loosened by the bath.

CARING FOR NAILS, EARS AND TEETH

Nails

Not all pet owners are comfortable trimming their dogs' nails, and not all dogs have been properly trained to accept it. Whether you tackle the job or turn it over to a groomer or veterinarian, the nails must be trimmed regularly: They are too long if they click on the ground when your dog walks.

Pay special attention to the dewclaws, the thumblike toenails higher on the foot. The dewclaws are removed from many newborn puppies, but when they are not, they can grow long and cut into the skin if not trimmed regularly.

If your dog won't let you handle his feet, don't force him or punish him too strictly. Call a groomer or a friend with a dog and either get help holding your dog or pay a groomer to clip his nails. If left unclipped, nails can grow to curl back under the toe. They can also cause the foot to splay, which can cause other skeletal and growth abnormalities.

Ears

The structure of the Siberian Husky's ear makes it relatively trouble-free for owners to care for. Nevertheless, the ears require routine monitoring, including weekly ear checks in which the owner examines the ears by sight and smell. It only takes a moment: Look inside for evidence of excessive brownish waxy buildup or discharge, then take a whiff. An unpleasant odor is often the first sign of ear problems. Once familiar with the

QUICK AND PAINLESS NAIL CLIPPING

This is possible if you make a habit out of handling your dog's feet and giving your dog treats when you do. When it's time to clip nails, go through the same routine, but take your clippers and snip off just the ends of the nail—clip too far down and you'll cut into the "quick," the nerve center, hurting your dog and causing the nail to bleed. Clip two nails a session while you're getting your dog used to the procedure, and you'll soon be doing all four feet quickly and easily.

scent of a healthy ear, one can more easily identify trouble should an infection begin to develop.

The Teeth

Your Husky puppy should have white, pearly teeth. So should your adult, but that isn't usually the case. Dogs, like people, are prone to the effects of poor dental hygiene—tartar and plaque buildup that leads to gingivitis, which leads to painful chewing and teeth that need to be pulled out.

Brushing your dog's teeth is easier than it sounds. The toughest part

By inspecting and brushing your dog's teeth regularly and getting a thorough professional cleaning from the veterinarian annually, your Husky should have pearly teeth all his life—and a lifetime of chewing.

is getting him used to you handling his mouth. The best way to do that is to work slowly—first lifting his gums for a few seconds while praising him, then lifting his gums, feeling his teeth, etc. When you and he are ready, use doggy toothpaste (never human toothpaste) or baking soda and a bit of water on a doggy toothbrush or a finger brush or on a gauze pad. Work the brush or pad around the teeth at the gum line, just like you do with your own teeth. Dogs like the taste of the doggy paste, and shouldn't mind the baking soda. That's it! No need to rinse.

TRADE SECRETS

Convincing your Siberian to comply with such seemingly odd practices as toothbrushing and nail clipping should begin as soon as possible in the pet and owner relationship. Keep the sessions short (try clipping only three or four nails per session, for example), reward your dog with a treat at the end of each grooming activity and keep things upbeat and positive. Such efforts, coupled with a healthy diet, will keep your Siberian Husky effervescent, inside and out.

CHAPTER SIX

Measuring Up

The Siberian Husky is a dog everyone knows. Although it is not *the* most popular pet, it is one of the most well-known dog breeds, even among those who really don't know dogs. The reason is simple: When someone offhandedly throws out the generic term "husky" or hears of a sled dog race in Alaska, invariably the image of the Siberian Husky, a blue-eyed dog that looks like a wolf, takes shape within the mind's eye.

Despite obvious similarities in appearance and a shared affinity for howling, the Siberian Husky is no closer to the wolf than is any other domestic dog. She does share, however, an intimate knowledge of the wilderness with her wild cousin, for both have evolved in some of the harshest, most remote regions on Earth.

Despite her great beauty and infectious smile, the Siberian Husky is one of those illustrious "fittest." Through human-assisted natural selection, she has proven she can happily survive almost anywhere. Yet the Siberian is shrouded in myth and legend, leaving modern humans to sort out what is real and what is fiction—something the Siberian owner must do if he or she is to become the partner this dog demands.

THE HUSKY'S HERITAGE

The Siberian Husky is an extremely adaptable pet— like this dog, who is ready for a backpacking trip.

A STRONG SURVIVOR

From such an environment has sprung a dog with speed, endurance and a friendly attitude that somehow belies the animal's great athletic ability. That dog is, of course, the Siberian Husky—the dog harnessed to a primitive sled, mushed by a fur-clad Eskimo across the frozen tundra, immortalized by Jack London in *The Call of the Wild*—the dog that carries our imaginations to the top of the world where only the fittest survive.

Although much of the Siberian's legend is just that, the truths of the breed at times seem mythological. The credit for these myths goes to the many people throughout history who have guided the breed's fate with wisdom and respect. Entrusted with a dog bred for an estimated 3,000 years by the Chukchis of Siberia, today's American breeders, armed with the American Kennel Club (AKC) Standard that dictates the ins and outs of Siberian breeding, continue to do justice to what those native breeders intended for their treasure. Were those ancient

Chukchis transported forward in time, they would probably have little trouble recognizing their dogs in a gathering of twentieth-century canines.

A Big Dog in a Not-So-Big Package

What might surprise the neophyte viewing a Siberian Husky for the first time is the dog's relatively small size. How could this diminutive, almost delicate creature be the grand dog of the north? The inspiration of countless adventure fantasies? Jack London's muse?

The Siberian Husky was designed for ultimate efficiency, that's how. What follows is a discussion of the physical characteristics of the Siberian Husky, based on the breed's Standard. For a copy of the official Standard, write to the American Kennel Club (see information in Chapter 9, "Resources").

HEIGHT—According to the official Standard of the breed as accepted by the American Kennel Club (AKC) and evident in most of the Siberians seen today, this high-powered

athlete should stand just under two feet at the withers. Specifically, females should stand 20 to 22 inches, males 21 to 23½ inches. Females should weigh 35 to 50 pounds, males 45 to 60 pounds.

The Siberian Husky is quite a bit smaller than the Alaskan Malamute, another wolfy-looking Arctic breed that, despite the dramatic size differences, is often mistaken for her smaller cousin and vice versa. Nevertheless, that smaller cousin continues to amaze

WHAT IS A BREED STANDARD?

A breed standard—a detailed description of an individual breed—is meant to portray the ideal specimen of that breed. This includes ideal structure, temperament, gait, type—all aspects of the dog. Because the standard describes an ideal specimen, it isn't based on any particular dog. It is a concept against which judges compare actual dogs, and breeders strive to produce dogs. At a dog show, the dog that wins is the one that comes closest, in the judge's opinion, to the standard for its breed. Breed standards are written by the breed parent clubs, the national organizations formed to oversee the well-being of the breed. They are voted on and approved by the members of the parent clubs.

This Siberian Husky (left) and Alaskan Malamute puppy (right) are almost identical in color, markings and wolflike features.

spectators and enthusiasts alike as one of the smallest, yet most capable dogs in the AKC's Working Group.

BUILD—The Siberian Husky is described in the Standard as a "medium-sized working dog, quick and light on its feet and free and graceful in action." It is precisely this image, one the dog readily embodies, that has drawn so many people from so many cultures to this breed.

Elegant and athletic, compact and well-balanced, the well-bred Siberian Husky cuts a sturdy figure with moderate bone and hard muscle, which facilitate the extraordinary strength and endurance for which the breed is known.

Engineered to move almost effortlessly across the snow and ice,

the Siberian boasts straight, parallel front legs with elbows held close to the body. The hindquarters are equally straight and parallel, the thighs rich with powerful muscle to propel the dog forward with balance and precision.

TAIL—Assisting in that mission is the tail, well-furred (though not too well-furred or too tightly curled) and carried over the back when the dog is alert and attentive. When relaxed, the Siberian's tail is dropped. When excited, no doubt when greeting either a known family member or a new acquaintance, the Siberian's tail wags wildly like a flag flying high above her back.

FEET—Whereas the tail adds balance and is a means of communicating moods, the structure of the Siberian's feet enables the dog to move in a way that makes one think the animal must surely be running on air. To keep the Siberian stepping lightly, those feet should be oval in shape and of medium size with thick, protective pads underneath and a dense growth of hair between the pads and toes, which provide the dog with traction and protection from frigid climates and rugged terrain. The Siberian can thus run tirelessly in the coldest of temperatures. To watch her move with such effortless grace is to witness the ideal marriage of agility and elegance.

BREATHTAKING BEAUTY

EYES—The Standard allows eyes that are brown, blue or even one of each. Parti-colored eyes are also acceptable. Look closely into those eyes, which have been known to unnerve if not outright frighten the uninitiated, and you may just note a hint of wanderlust smoldering within.

HEAD—Even with those mysterious eyes, the Siberian's expression is one of energy and exuberance and even,

as the Standard suggests, projects an element of mischief.

The Siberian's profile resembles that of the wolf: her muzzle medium in width, tapered to the nose; the triangular-shaped, well-furred ears with softly rounded tips positioned high on her head, alert to any new and exciting sound; teeth closed in a

THE AMERICAN KENNEL CLUB

Familiarly referred to as "the AKC," the American Kennel Club is a nonprofit organization devoted to the advancement of purebred dogs. The AKC maintains a registry of recognized breeds and adopts and enforces rules for dog events including shows, obedience trials, field trials, hunting tests, lure coursing, herding, earth-dog trials, agility and the Canine Good Citizen program. It is a club of clubs, established in 1884 and composed, today, of over 500 autonomous dog clubs throughout the United States. Each club is represented by a delegate; the delegates make up the legislative body of the AKC, voting on rules and electing directors. The American Kennel Club maintains the Stud Book, the record of every dog ever registered with the AKC, and publishes a variety of materials on purebred dogs, including a monthly magazine, books and numerous educational pamphlets. For more information, contact the AKC at the address listed in Chapter 9, "Resources."

53

The Husky's eyes are just as beautiful in brown.

54

For most people, it's the Siberian's glacier-blue eyes that first capture their attention.

scissors bite, except when the jaw is open in the traditional Siberian smile.

COAT—Also unforgettable is the Siberian Husky's thick, medium-length double coat, a veritable feat of both beauty and engineering that is common to all of the northern breeds. Consisting of a soft, fluffy undercoat close to the skin covered by a sea of coarser, longer guard hairs, these two layers work in concert to insulate the dog naturally from even subzero temperatures.

When faced with such temperatures, the hair follicles in the dog's coat respond by standing erect to trap and, with the body's natural heat, warm the air in the thick undercoat. The guard hairs also protect the skin from vegetation and other environmental irritants, and as an added bonus, the coat rarely emits the doggy odor common to so many other members of the canine species. Indeed, the Siberian is a very clean breed, and she generally strives to maintain her own cleanliness almost as diligently as does a cat.

COLORS—Apart from its obvious value in protecting the dog from the elements, the Siberian's coat is aesthetically irresistible as well. According to the Standard, all colors are allowed, from black to pure white (colors that determine what color the dog's nose will be), but Siberians are most frequently found in shimmering red and white, black and white, gray and white and copper and white.

This attractive coat may be complemented by a raccoon-like bandit mask that marks the face of many a Siberian. Like snowflakes, no two Siberian Huskies share identical patterns and markings. No two are alike.

WELL-BALANCED SOUL

Also unique is the Siberian Husky's disposition, which, like the dog's size, may also surprise those who have come to know sled dogs solely through Jack London's books. In other words, despite what Mr. London's tales may tell us, this is no vicious fighting dog, no incorruptible warrior. The Siberian Husky loves everyone, and her mission in life is to ensure that everyone knows it.

The mysterious parti-colored eyes (one brown and one blue) are also acceptable according to the Standard.

At first glance one might mistake this profile for a wolf's.

55

TEMPERAMENT—The well-bred Siberian Husky is balanced in both physique and disposition. As the breed's Standard emphasizes, the Siberian's temperament is just as

A red-and-white Siberian Husky.

critical to the dog's identity as are her distinctive physical attributes. Furthermore, that temperament must be friendlier and gentler than any human being could ever hope to have.

Don't expect quintessential guard-dog behavior from your Siberian. This dog is driven to share all she has and all her owner has with anyone and everyone she happens to meet. Friendly, outgoing, gentle and alert are the words used to describe the ideal Siberian

56

A silver-and-white Siberian Husky.

character. The Siberian in turn takes these concepts to heart as her birthright.

Your Siberian Husky should display an inherent *joie de vivre*—boundless energy indicative of a true love for life. She is a gregarious animal, raised traditionally for deadly serious work in a region where all members of the tribe, both canine and human, knew their lives hung by a thread every day. Yet the Siberian reveled in her work and in her close relationship with the people and other dogs with whom she lived and survived.

57

THE ULTIMATE TEAM PLAYER

The Siberian was developed, and very successfully so, to be the ultimate team player. She thrives best in the company of people whose greatest joy is to spend a great deal of time with their dogs—and in the company of other dogs, too, a perspective no doubt sculpted by the dog's spending centuries in the pack in frigid Siberia.

The Siberian Husky, however, is not clingy or constantly hungry for human acceptance. Such a suggestion would elicit peals of laughter from any seasoned Siberian enthusiast. This dog is independent with a stubborn intelligence that can easily try the patience of even the most experienced dog trainer. Yet the Siberian will both obey and disobey with equal gusto and humor—behavior that may not be so eagerly shared by those trying to direct the dog's energy and actions into institutionalized patterns of obedience.

The Siberian is nevertheless quite sensitive to the rules of the

A raccoonlike bandit mask complements the parti-colored eyes of this black-and-white Husky.

The Siberian Husky loves everyone and will display her affection proudly.

pack—historically, she had to be to survive. While she thus extends her affection to all, she reserves her respect for only the few who earn it. One way to earn that respect is to be a firm yet gentle leader and to provide the dog with ample opportunity for adventure. As her variegated history demonstrates, the Siberian Husky, when led by a worthy leader, has always adapted well to every new situation. This adaptability is a vital facet of this ancient breed.

CHAPTER SEVEN

A Matter of Fact

For most, the thought of exile in Siberia is a nightmare. For the Siberian Husky, it is home.

This barren region of ice and snow, where countless political prisoners were sent as a cruel and unusual form of punishment, was also historically the native land of the Chukchis. That we know of these people and that they remained in the region for thousands of years is a testament to the dog that made it all happen. Without their dogs—dogs that would ultimately be named the Siberian Husky—their culture, their people, probably would not have survived.

Dog historians believe that the northern breeds—Siberian Husky, Alaskan Malamute, Samoyed and so forth—all shared a common ancestor (whether or not that ancestor was the wolf is a subject for debate

The Siberian Husky is known as a Nordic dog and a member of the American Kennel Club's Working Group of dogs.

that will probably never be settled). Canine historian Maxwell Riddle has spoken of the "family of the northern forest," the dogs that would become our modern Nordic dogs. With such a family in their background, these breeds, though retaining certain like characteristics, diverged into their distinctive types, based on the various people who nurtured them and according to the demands of their owners' specific climates and terrain and their subsequent needs in sled dogs.

CHUKCHI DOGS

For the Chukchis, this meant developing a dog that would meet the very specific demands of their environment and lifestyle. The Chukchis lived in permanent settlements inland but had to travel long distances to the coast to hunt. What they then sought in their ultimate dog was a smallish, fast animal who could transport relatively light loads over long distances in the extreme subzero temperatures of northeast Asia. This dog also needed an extraordinarily efficient metabolism that, due to food limitations, could be sufficiently fueled on less food than one might expect for such a hardworking animal.

Equally important to the Chukchis was the dog's amenability to working in large teams; given the size of the dogs, the heavier the sled loads became, the more dogs the hunters would add to the team.

When we review the ancient lifestyle that led to the development of the Siberian Husky, and view the modern-day representatives of the breed, we see little difference in the dog that ancient cultures created for their specific needs and the dog that still lives among us today.

Although life for those early Siberians—both human and canine—was harsh, the Chukchis exhibited a wisdom in their breeding practices that we would be wise to emulate today. They bred selectively for temperament as well as for physical characteristics, which explains why the Siberian Huskies are today legendary for their ability and willingness to work so well with both humans and other dogs—and their demands to be integral members of the family.

A True Coexistence

For obvious reasons, the Chukchis grew to depend on their dogs. On the trail, they learned to trust their dogs' instincts, a trust modern-day Siberian Huskies continue to demand from those who choose to take to the trail with them. At

WHERE DID DOGS COME FROM?

It can be argued that dogs were right there at man's side from the beginning of time. As soon as human beings began to document their existence, the dog was among their drawings and inscriptions. Dogs were not just friends, they served a purpose: There were dogs to hunt birds, pull sleds, herd sheep, burrow after rats—even sit in laps! What your dog was originally bred to do influences the way he behaves. The American Kennel Club recognizes over 140 breeds, and there are hundreds more distinct breeds around the world. To make sense of the breeds, they are grouped according to their size or function. The AKC has seven groups:

1. Sporting
2. Working
3. Herding
4. Hounds
5. Terriers
6. Toys
7. Non Sporting

Can you name a breed from each group? Here's some help: (1) Golden Retriever, (2) Doberman Pinscher, (3) Collie, (4) Beagle, (5) Scottish Terrier, (6) Maltese, and (7) Dalmatian. All modern domestic dogs (*Canis familiaris*) are related, however different they look, and are all descended from *Canis lupus*, the gray wolf.

Siberian Huskies are legendary for their ability and willingness to work well with humans and other dogs.

like the Chukchis, to listen to their dogs.

In the time line of the Siberian's story, the dog was bred first for utility purposes and, therefore, for the survival of his people. This purpose established a foundation for the Siberian's future, a stability that would be instantly recognized by those who would meet the dog in the years ahead and ensure that he would survive the changes in lifestyle he would inevitably encounter.

SLED DOG RACING

It was within this atmosphere that Siberians ran their first recorded major race. It occurred in 1908 in the 408-mile All-Alaska Sweepstakes Race. The newcomers, mushed by someone unfamiliar with them, didn't win, but they made a great showing and attracted the attention of all spectators—including the gamblers in the crowd. From then on, the Siberian Husky took this budding sport by storm and within a few short years had become Alaska's premier racer.

Originally christened the Chukchi Husky—"husky" being a generic term for "sled pulling

home, the dogs enjoyed an intimate involvement with their families, a bond that was strengthened because every member of the family, children and adults alike, was responsible for caring for the lifeline that was the dog team.

This unique relationship between dog and family thus elevated coexistence to a symbiotic art form all its own. The two species learned to read and understand each other's body language, and the Siberian Husky's instincts, forged through that bond, have since saved countless lives on the trail—lives of people who have learned, dog"—this newcomer to Alaska was obsessive about running and was long accustomed to hard work. The dog was thus the ideal candidate to get in on the dawn of sled dog racing at the beginning of the twentieth century. Although some onlookers originally scoffed at the dogs' size, their scoffs turned to praise as the breed proved their mettle and quickly earned a broad following.

Spectators and mushers alike admired Siberians for their speed, endurance, manageability and beauty. The dogs, meanwhile, took to racing and the sheer joy of running just for the fun of it, as though they knew this was the destiny for which they had been preparing for the past 3,000 years.

SHOW DOG/ WORK DOG

With a reputation that was growing by leaps and bounds, the Siberian Husky was granted recognition by the American Kennel Club (AKC) in the 1930s. He has since enjoyed many hours of thunderous applause from dog show audiences, but all has not been fame and glitter for the twentieth-century Siberian Husky.

63

When a Husky is told to mush, he interprets that as a command to run faster. This Husky is wearing a weight-pulling harness, but doesn't look like he's much in the mood for mushing.

THE ESSENTIAL SIBERIAN HUSKY

During the early years of the twentieth century, the dogs were still called on from time to time for their Chukchi-born skills and uses.

The Siberian Husky's career has included transporting mail in Alaska and Canada when, until the advent of the snowmobile and bush plane, dog team was the only way the mail could get through. The Siberian has pulled children by dog sled to school when a snowed-in schoolhouse was otherwise inaccessible, and he even served as a search and rescue dog in the Arctic during World War II. But the most profound example of the Siberian's role in serious work occurred in 1925 with the Great Serum Run.

THE GREAT SERUM RUN

In the winter of that year, a diphtheria epidemic broke out in Nome, Alaska. Although a serum existed

for the illness, there was no way of getting it from Anchorage to that distant point—until someone thought of enlisting the services of Leonhard Seppala, a Norwegian immigrant who had become one of Alaska's premier mushers. His dog of choice—the Siberian Husky.

Seppala called his and many other teams throughout the territory to action, teams that were invariably dominated by Siberian Huskies. What ensued was a lifesaving relay of dog teams through the Alaskan interior.

The news spread south, and practically overnight the art of mushing had become immortal throughout the world (including a lead dog named Balto, whose statue now stands in New York's Central Park). The Great Serum Run is still commemorated each year in Alaska with the running of the "Iditarod" from Anchorage to Nome.

THE TWENTIETH CENTURY HUSKY

Today the Siberian enjoys a career of many facets. He remains a powerful and very popular sled dog but has found contentment with people who neither want nor need to travel by

FAMOUS OWNERS OF SIBERIAN HUSKIES

Kate Jackson	Burt Ward
Jessica Savitch	Carole Lombard

64

dog sled. He has become a popular show dog say those and a valued partner in such recreational activities as cross-country skiing, skijoring (an activity in which a single dog pulls a person on skis) and virtually any other sport in which dogs play active roles.

A NATURAL MUSHER

Mushing remains the Siberian's greatest calling, of course, and he has entered the increasingly popular world of recreational mushing with a vengeance. As new owners discover the addictive properties of the breed and realize they simply must own more than one, recreational mushing, where they may put their dogs to work together in the calling for which they were bred, is the next logical step.

On a more formal level, the Siberian excels best in mid-distance races, often in teams as large as twenty dogs. Because of the breed's size and special talents, they just naturally work well together.

Those unfamiliar with the art of mushing and the dogs who love it are often inclined to place

Then, as now, the Siberian sports a friendly, smiling face. Then, as now, he recognizes serious business and his role in it.

themselves in what they believe to be the sled dog's booties (paw-sized slippers the dogs wear in extreme conditions) and deem the sport cruel. The dogs, of course, have a different opinion, evident in the wails of joy that emerge as soon as the musher approaches the team with harness in hand.

Cruel treatment in the Siberian's eyes is being the dog who is left at home. Pulling a sled through the snow with a team of his best friends, his human leader at the helm, is what the Siberian Husky was born for. For some, it is what they live for. This was true for their ancestors, and it holds true just as profoundly today.

CHAPTER EIGHT

On Good Behavior

by Ian Dunbar, Ph.D., MRCVS

Training is the jewel in the crown—the most important aspect of doggy husbandry. There is no more important variable influencing dog behavior and temperament than the dog's education: A well-trained, well-behaved and good-natured puppydog is always a joy to live with, but an untrained and uncivilized dog can be a perpetual nightmare. Moreover, deny the dog an education and she will not have the opportunity to fulfill her own canine potential;

neither will she have the ability to communicate effectively with her human companions.

Luckily, modern psychological training methods are easy, efficient, effective and, above all, considerably dog-friendly and user-friendly. Doggy education is as simple as it is enjoyable. But before you can have a good time play-training with your new dog, you have to learn what to do and how to do it. There is no bigger variable influencing the success of dog training than the owner's experience and expertise. Before you embark on the dog's education, you must first educate yourself.

This owner knew before she adopted her Siberian Husky that the breed required an enormous amount of physical activity and training, which has made life with her pet more fulfilling.

67

BASIC TRAINING FOR OWNERS

Ideally, basic owner training should begin well before you select your dog. Find out all you can about your chosen breed first, then master rudimentary training and handling skills. If you already have your puppydog, owner training is a dire emergency—the clock is ticking! Especially for puppies, the first few weeks at home are the most important and influential days in the dog's life. Indeed, the cause of most adolescent and adult problems may be traced back to the initial days the pup explores her new home. This is the time to establish the *status quo*— to teach the puppydog how you would like her to behave and so prevent otherwise quite predictable problems.

In addition to consulting breeders and breed books such as this one (which understandably have a positive breed bias), seek out as many pet owners with your breed as you can find. Good points are obvious. What you want to find out are the breed-specific problems, so you can nip them in the bud. In particular, you should talk to owners with adolescent dogs and make a list of all anticipated problems. Most important, test drive at least half a dozen adolescent and adult dogs of your breed yourself. An 8-week-old puppy is deceptively easy to handle, but she will acquire adult size, speed and strength in just four months, so you should learn now what to prepare for.

Puppy and pet dog training classes offer a convenient venue to locate pet owners and observe dogs in action. For a list of suitable trainers in your area, contact the Association of Pet Dog Trainers at (800) PET-DOGS.

PRINCIPLES OF TRAINING

Most people think training comprises teaching the dog to do things such as sit, speak and roll over, but even a 4-week-old pup knows how to do these things already. Instead, the first step in training involves teaching the dog human words for each dog behavior and activity and for each aspect of the dog's environment. That way you, the owner, can more easily participate in the dog's domestic education by directing her to perform specific actions

appropriately, that is, at the right time, in the right place and so on. Training opens communication channels, enabling an educated dog to at least understand her owner's requests.

In addition to teaching a dog what we want her to do, it is also necessary to teach her why she should do what we ask. Indeed, 95 percent of training revolves around motivating the dog to want to do what we want. Dogs often understand what their owners want; they just don't see the point of doing it—especially when the owner's repetitively boring and seemingly senseless instructions are totally at odds with much more pressing and exciting doggy distractions. It is not so much the dog that is being stubborn or dominant; rather, it is the owner who has failed to acknowledge the dog's needs and feelings and to approach training from the dog's point of view.

The Meaning of Instructions

The secret to successful training is learning how to use training lures to predict or prompt specific behaviors—to coax the dog to do what you want when you want. Any highly valued object (such as a treat or toy) may be used as a lure, which the dog will follow with her eyes and nose. Moving the lure in specific ways entices the dog to move her nose, head and entire body in specific ways. In fact, by learning the art of manipulating various lures, it is possible to teach the dog to assume virtually any body position and perform any action. Once you have control over the expression of the dog's behaviors and can elicit any body position or behavior at will, you can easily teach the dog to perform on request.

Tell your dog what you want her to do, use a lure to entice her to respond correctly, then profusely praise and maybe reward her once she performs the desired action. For example, verbally request "Fido, sit!" while you move a squeaky toy upwards and backwards over the dog's muzzle (lure-movement and hand signal), smile knowingly as she looks up (to follow the lure) and sits down (as a result of canine anatomical engineering), then praise her to distraction ("Gooood Fido!"). Squeak the toy, offer a training treat and give your dog and yourself a pat on the back.

OWNING A PARTY ANIMAL

It's a fact: The more of the world your puppy is exposed to, the more comfortable she'll be in it. Once your puppy's had her shots, start taking her everywhere with you. Encourage friendly interaction with strangers, expose her to different environments (towns, fields, beaches) and most important, enroll her in a puppy class where she'll get to play with other puppies. These simple, fun, shared activities will develop your pup into a confident socialite; reliable around other people and dogs.

69

Being able to elicit desired responses over and over enables the owner to reward the dog over and over. Consequently, the dog begins to think training is fun. For example, the more the dog is rewarded for sitting, the more she enjoys sitting. Eventually the dog comes to realize that, whereas most sitting is appreciated, sitting immediately upon request usually prompts especially enthusiastic praise and a slew of high-level rewards. The dog begins to sit on cue much of the time, showing that she is starting to grasp the meaning of the owner's verbal request and hand signal.

The word train-ing may sound tedious to the human ear, but for dogs, train-ing means it's time to use their brains.

70

Why Comply?

Most dogs enjoy initial lure-reward training and are only too happy to comply with their owners' wishes. Unfortunately, repetitive drilling without appreciative feedback tends to diminish the dog's enthusiasm until she eventually fails to see the point of complying anymore. Moreover, as the dog approaches adolescence she becomes more easily distracted as she develops other interests. Lengthy sessions with repetitive exercises tend to bore and demotivate both parties. If it's not fun, the owner doesn't do it and

neither does the dog. Integrate training into your dog's life: The greater number of training sessions each day and the shorter they are, the more willingly compliant your dog will become.

TRAINER'S TOOLS

Many training books extol the virtues of a vast array of training paraphernalia. In reality, most effec-tive training tools are not found in stores; they come from within our-selves. In addition to a willing dog, all you really need is a functional human brain, gentle hands, a loving heart and a good attitude.

In terms of equipment, all dogs do require a quality buckle collar to sport dog tags and to attach the leash (for safety and to comply with local leash laws). Hollow chew toys (like Kongs or sterilized longbones) and a dog bed or collapsible crate are musts for housetraining. Three additional tools are required:

1. specific lures (training treats and toys) to predict and prompt spe-cific desired behaviors;

2. rewards (praise, affection, train-ing treats and toys) to reinforce for the dog what a lot of fun it all is; and

3. knowledge—how to convert the dog's favorite activities and games (potential distractions to training) into "life-rewards," which may be employed to facilitate training.

The most powerful of these is knowledge. Education is the key!

HOUSETRAINING

If dogs were left to their own devices, certainly they would chew, dig and bark for entertainment and then no doubt highlight a few areas of their living space with sprinkles of urine, in much the same way we decorate by hanging pictures. Consequently, when we ask a dog to live with us, we must teach her *where* she may dig, *where* she may perform her toilet duties, *what* she may chew and *when* she may bark. After all, when left at home alone for many hours, we cannot expect the dog to amuse herself by completing crosswords or watching the soaps on TV!

Also, it would be decidedly unfair to keep the house rules a secret from the dog, and then get angry and punish the poor critter for inevitably transgressing rules she did

not even know existed. Remember: Without adequate education and guidance, the dog will be forced to establish her own rules—doggy rules—and most probably will be at odds with the owner's view of domestic living.

Since most problems develop during the first few days the dog is at home, prospective dog owners must be certain they are quite clear about the principles of housetraining *before* they get a dog. Early misbehaviors quickly become established as the *status quo*—becoming firmly entrenched as hard-to-break bad

Rewarding your Siberian Husky when she does something good will aid in teaching her to continue that behavior, such as sitting on command.

habits, which set the precedent for years to come. Make sure to teach your dog good habits right from the start. Good habits are just as hard to break as bad ones!

Ideally, when a new dog comes home, try to arrange for someone to be present as much as possible during the first few days (for adult dogs) or weeks for puppies. With only a little forethought, it is surprisingly easy to find a puppy sitter, such as a retired person, who would be willing to eat from your refrigerator and watch your television while keeping an eye on the newcomer to encourage the dog to play with chew toys and to ensure she goes outside on a regular basis.

Punishing your Siberian Husky will cause her to be confused and unwilling to learn.

Potty Training

To teach the dog where to relieve herself:

1. never let her make a single mistake;

2. let her know where you want her to go; and

3. handsomely reward her for doing so: "GOOOOOOOD DOG!!!" liver treat, liver treat, liver treat!

Preventing Mistakes

A single mistake is a training disaster, since it heralds many more in future weeks. And each time the dog soils the house, this further reinforces the dog's unfortunate preference for an indoor, carpeted toilet. Do not let an unhousetrained dog have full run of the house.

When you are away from home, or cannot pay full attention, confine the dog to an area where elimination is appropriate, such as an outdoor run or, better still, a small, comfortable indoor kennel with access to an outdoor run. When confined in this

manner, most dogs will naturally housetrain themselves.

If that's not possible, confine the dog to an area, such as a utility room, kitchen, basement or garage, where elimination may not be desired in the long run but as an interim measure it is certainly preferable to doing it all around the house. Use newspaper to cover the floor of the dog's day room. The newspaper may be used to soak up the urine and to wrap up and dispose of the feces. Once your dog develops a preferred spot for eliminating, it is only necessary to cover that part of the floor with newspaper. The smaller papered area may then be moved (only a little each day) towards the door to the outside. Thus the dog will develop the tendency to go to the door when she needs to relieve herself.

Never confine an unhousetrained dog to a crate for long periods. Doing so would force the dog to soil the crate and ruin its usefulness as an aid for housetraining (see the following discussion).

Teaching Where

In order to teach your dog where you would like her to do her

HOUSETRAINING 1-2-3

1. Prevent Mistakes. When you can't supervise your puppy, confine her in a single room or in her crate (but don't leave her for too long!). Puppy-proof the area by laying down newspapers so that if she does make a mistake, it won't matter.

2. Teach Where. Take your puppy to the spot you want her to use every hour.

3. When she goes, praise her profusely and give her three favorite treats.

73

business, you have to be there to direct the proceedings—an obvious, yet often neglected, fact of life. In order to be there to teach the dog where to go, you need to know *when* she needs to go. Indeed, the success of housetraining depends on the owner's ability to predict these times. Certainly, a regular feeding schedule will facilitate prediction somewhat, but there is nothing like "loading the deck" and influencing the timing of the outcome yourself!

Whenever you are at home, make sure the dog is under constant supervision and/or confined to a small area. If already well trained, simply instruct the dog to lie down

Your new puppy needs supervision to stay out of trouble.

in her bed or basket. Alternatively, confine the dog to a crate (doggy den) or tie-down (a short, 18-inch lead that can be clipped to an eye hook in the baseboard near her bed). Short-term close confinement strongly inhibits urination and defecation, since the dog does not want to soil her sleeping area. Thus, when you release the puppydog each hour, she will definitely need to urinate immediately and defecate every third or fourth hour. Keep the dog confined to her doggy den and take her to her intended toilet area each hour, every hour and on the hour. When taking your dog outside,

instruct her to sit quietly before opening the door—she will soon learn to sit by the door when she needs to go out!

Teaching Why

Being able to predict when the dog needs to go enables the owner to be on the spot to praise and reward the dog. Each hour, hurry the dog to the intended toilet area in the yard, issue the appropriate instruction ("Go pee!" or "Go poop!"), then give the dog three to four minutes to produce. Praise and offer a couple of training treats when successful. The treats are important because many people fail to praise their dogs with feeling . . . and housetraining is hardly the time for understatement. So either loosen up and enthusiastically praise that dog: "Wuzzer-wuzzer-wuzzer, hooooser good wuffer den? Hoooo went pee for Daddy?" Or say "Good dog!" as best you can and offer the treats for effect.

Following elimination is an ideal time for a spot of play-training in the yard or house. Also, an empty dog may be allowed greater freedom around the house for the next half hour or so, just as long as you keep an eye out to make sure she does not get into other kinds of mischief. If you are preoccupied and cannot pay full attention, confine the dog to her doggy den once more to enjoy a peaceful snooze or to play with her many chew toys.

If your dog does not eliminate within the allotted time outside—no biggie! Back to her doggy den, and then try again after another hour.

Beware of falling into the trap of walking the dog to get her to eliminate. The good ol' dog walk is such an enormous highlight in the dog's life that it represents the single biggest potential reward in domestic dogdom. However, when in a hurry, or during inclement weather, many owners abruptly terminate the walk the moment the dog has done her business. This, in effect, severely punishes the dog for doing the right thing, in the right place at the right time. Consequently, many dogs become strongly inhibited from eliminating outdoors because they know it will signal an abrupt end to an otherwise thoroughly enjoyable walk.

Instead, instruct the dog to relieve herself in the yard prior to going for a walk. If you follow the above instructions, most dogs soon learn to eliminate on cue. As soon as

the dog eliminates, praise (and offer a treat or two)—"Good dog! Let's go walkies!" Use the walk as a reward for eliminating in the yard. If the dog does not go, put her back in her doggy den and think about a walk later on. You will find with a "No feces—no walk" policy, your dog will become one of the fastest defecators in the business.

If you do not have a backyard, instruct the dog to eliminate right outside your front door prior to the walk. Not only will this facilitate clean up and disposal of the feces in your own trash can but, also, the walk may again be used as a colossal reward.

75

A crate is multi-functional. It's a close confine-ment area, a safe pet carrier and sleeping and eating quarters all wrapped up in one!

COME AND SIT

Most puppies will happily approach virtually anyone, whether called or not; that is, until they collide with adolescence and develop other more important doggy interests, such as sniffing a multiplicity of exquisite odors on the grass. Your mission is to teach and reward the pup for coming reliably, willingly and happily when called—and you have just three months to get it done. Unless adequately reinforced, your puppy's tendency to approach people will self-destruct by adolescence.

Call your dog ("Fido, come!"), open your arms (and maybe squat down) as a welcoming signal, waggle

TOYS THAT EARN THEIR KEEP

To entertain even the most distracted of dogs, while you're home or away, have a selection of the following toys on hand: hollow chew toys (like Kongs, sterilized hollow longbones and cubes or balls that can be stuffed with kibble). Smear peanut butter or honey on the inside of the hollow toy or bone and stuff the bone with kibble and your dog will think of nothing else but working the object to get at the food. Great to take your dog's mind off the fact that you've left the house.

a treat or toy as a lure and reward the puppydog when she comes running. Do not wait to praise the dog until she reaches you—she may come 95 percent of the way and then run off after some distraction. Instead, praise the dog's first step towards you and continue praising enthusiastically for every step she takes in your direction.

When the rapidly approaching puppy dog is three lengths away from impact, instruct her to sit ("Fido, sit!") and hold the lure in front of you in an outstretched hand to prevent her from hitting you mid-chest and knocking you flat on your back! As Fido decelerates to nose the lure, move the treat upwards and backwards just over her muzzle with an upwards motion of your extended arm (palm-upwards). As the dog looks up to follow the lure, she will sit down (if she jumps up, you are holding the lure too high). Praise the dog for sitting. Move backwards and call her again. Repeat this many times over, always praising when Fido comes and sits; on occasion, reward her.

For the first couple of trials, use a training treat both as a lure to entice the dog to come and sit and as a reward for doing so. Thereafter,

Introducing your puppy to the chew toy will keep her from chewing up your shoes, and chewing the toy will certainly remain your pet's favorite hobby into her adult years.

try to use different items as lures and rewards. For example, lure the dog with a Kong or Frisbee but reward her with a food treat. Or lure the dog with a food treat but pat her and throw a tennis ball as a reward. After just a few repetitions, dispense with the lures and rewards; the dog will begin to respond willingly to your verbal requests and hand signals just for the prospect of praise from your heart and affection from your hands.

Even though your dog quickly masters obedient recalls in the house, her reliability may falter when playing in the backyard or local park. Ironically, it is the owner who has unintentionally trained the dog not to respond in these instances. By allowing the dog to play and run around and otherwise have a good time, but then to call the dog to put her on leash to take her home, the dog quickly learns playing is fun but training is a drag. Thus, playing in the park becomes a severe distraction, which works against training. Bad news!

Instead, whether playing with the dog off leash or on leash, request her to come at frequent intervals— say, every minute or so. On most occasions, praise and pet the dog for a few seconds while she is sitting, then tell her to go play again. For especially fast recalls, offer a couple of training treats and take the time to praise and pet the dog enthusiastically before releasing her. The dog will learn that coming when called is not necessarily the end of the play session, and neither is it the end of the world; rather, it signals an enjoyable, quality time-out with the owner before resuming play once more. In fact, playing in the park now becomes a very effective life-reward, which works to facilitate training by reinforcing each obedient and timely recall. Good news!

SIT, DOWN, STAND AND ROLLOVER

Teaching the dog a variety of body positions is easy for owner and dog, impressive for spectators and extremely useful for all. Using lure-reward techniques, it is possible to train several positions at once to verbal commands or hand signals (which impress the socks off onlookers).

Sit and down—the two control commands—prevent or resolve nearly a hundred behavior problems. For example, if the dog happily and obediently sits or lies down when requested, she cannot jump on visitors, dash out the front door, run around and chase her tail, pester other dogs, harass cats or annoy family, friends or strangers. Additionally, "Sit" or "Down" are the best emergency commands for off-leash control.

It is easier to teach and maintain a reliable sit than maintain a reliable recall. Sit is the purest and simplest of commands—either the dog is sitting or she is not. If there is any change of circumstances or potential danger in the park, for example, simply instruct the dog to sit. If she sits, you have a number of options: Allow the dog to resume playing when she is safe, walk up and put the dog on leash or call the dog. The dog will be much more likely to come when called if she has already acknowledged her compliance by sitting. If the dog does not sit in the park—train her to!

Stand and rollover-stay are the two positions for examining the dog. Your veterinarian will love you to distraction if you take a little time to teach the dog to stand still and roll over and play possum. Also, your vet bills will be smaller because it will take the veterinarian less time to examine your dog. The rollover-stay is an especially useful command and is really just a variation of the down-stay: Whereas the dog lies prone in the traditional down, she lies supine in the rollover-stay.

As with teaching come and sit, the training techniques to teach the dog to assume all other body positions on cue are user-friendly and dog-friendly. Simply give the appropriate request, lure the dog into the desired body position using a training treat or toy and then praise (and maybe reward) the dog as soon as she complies. Try not to touch the dog to get her to respond. If you teach the dog by guiding her into position, the dog will quickly learn that rump-pressure means sit, for example, but as yet you still have no control over your dog if she is just 6 feet away. It will still be necessary to teach the dog to sit on request. So do not make training a time-consuming two-step process; instead, teach the dog to sit to a verbal request or hand signal from the outset. Once the dog sits willingly when requested, by all means use your hands to pet the dog when she does so.

To teach down when the dog is already sitting, say "Fido, down!," hold the lure in one hand (palm down) and lower that hand to the

FINDING A TRAINER

Have fun with your dog, take a training class! But don't just sign on any dotted line, find a trainer whose approach and style you like and whose students (and their dogs) are really learning. Ask to visit a class to observe a trainer in action. For the names of trainers near you, ask your veterinarian, your pet supply store, your dog-owning neighbors or call (800) PET-DOGS (the Association of Pet Dog Trainers).

floor between the dog's forepaws. As the dog lowers her head to follow the lure, slowly move the lure away from the dog just a fraction (in front of her paws). The dog will lie down as she stretches her nose forward to follow the lure. Praise the dog when she does so. If the dog stands up, you pulled the lure away too far and too quickly.

When teaching the dog to lie down from the standing position, say "Down" and lower the lure to the floor as before. Once the dog has lowered her forequarters and assumed a play bow, gently and slowly move the lure towards the dog between her forelegs. Praise the dog as soon as her rear end plops down.

You will notice the more energetically you move your arm—upwards (palm up) to get the dog to sit, and downwards (palm down) to get the dog to lie down—the more energetically the dog responds to your requests. Now try training the dog in silence and you will notice she has also learned to respond to hand signals. Yeah! Not too shabby for the first session.

To teach stand from the sitting position, say "Fido, stand," slowly move the lure half a dog-length away from the dog's nose, keeping it at nose level, and praise the dog as she stands to follow the lure. As soon as the dog stands, lower the lure to just beneath the dog's chin to entice her to look down; otherwise she will stand and then sit immediately. To prompt the dog to stand from the down position, move the lure half a dog-length upwards and away from the dog, holding the lure at standing nose height from the floor.

Teaching rollover is best started from the down position, with the dog lying on one side, or at least with both hind legs stretched out on the same side. Say "Fido, bang!" and move the lure backwards and alongside the dog's muzzle to her elbow (on the side of her outstretched hind legs). Once the dog looks to the side and backwards, very slowly move the lure upwards to the dog's shoulder and backbone. Tickling the dog in the goolies (groin area) often invokes a reflex-raising of the hind leg as an appeasement gesture, which facilitates the tendency to roll over. If you move the lure too quickly and the dog jumps into the standing position, have patience and start again. As soon as the dog rolls onto her back, keep the lure stationary and mesmerize the dog with a relaxing tummy rub.

Your well-trained Siberian Husky will be the apple of your eye.

80

To teach rollover-stay when the dog is standing or moving, say "Fido, bang!" and give the appropriate hand signal (with index finger pointed and thumb cocked in true Sam Spade fashion), then in one fluid movement lure her to first lie down and then rollover-stay as above.

Teaching the dog to stay in each of the above four positions becomes a piece of cake after first teaching the dog not to worry at the toy or treat training lure. This is best accomplished by hand feeding dinner kibble. Hold a piece of kibble firmly in your hand and softly instruct "Off!" Ignore any licking and slobbering for however long the dog worries at the treat, but say "Take it!" and offer the kibble *the instant* the dog breaks contact with her muzzle. Repeat this a few times, and then up the ante and insist the dog remove her muzzle for one whole second before offering the kibble. Then progressively refine your criteria and have the dog not touch your hand (or treat) for longer and longer periods on each trial, such as for two seconds, four seconds, then six, ten, fifteen, twenty, thirty seconds and so on.

The dog soon learns: (1) worrying at the treat never gets results, whereas (2) noncontact is often rewarded after a variable time lapse.

Teaching "Off!" has many useful applications in its own right. Additionally, instructing the dog not to touch a training lure often produces spontaneous and magical stays. Request the dog to stand-stay, for example, and not to touch the lure. At first set your sights on a short two-second stay before rewarding the dog. (Remember, every long journey begins with a single step.) However, on subsequent trials, gradually and progressively increase the length of stay required to receive a reward. In no time at all your dog will stand calmly for a minute or so.

RELEVANCY TRAINING

Once you have taught the dog what you expect her to do when requested to come, sit, lie down, stand, rollover and stay, the time is right to teach the dog why she should comply with your wishes. The secret is to have many extremely short training interludes (two to five seconds each) at numerous times during the course of the dog's day.

In no time at all the dog will be only too pleased to follow your instructions because she has learned that a compliant response heralds all sorts of goodies. Basically all you are trying to teach the dog is how to say please: "Please throw the tennis ball. Please may I snuggle on the couch."

In fact, the dog may be unable to distinguish between training and good times and, indeed, there should be no distinction. The warped concept that training involves forcing the dog to comply

and/or dominating her will is totally at odds with the picture of a truly well-trained dog. In reality, enjoying a game of training with a dog is no different from enjoying a game of backgammon or tennis with a friend; and walking with a dog should be no different from strolling with a spouse, or with buddies on the golf course.

WALK BY YOUR SIDE

Many people attempt to teach a dog to heel by putting her on a leash and physically correcting the dog when she makes mistakes. There are a number of things seriously wrong with this approach, the first being that most people do not want precision heeling; rather, they simply want the dog to follow or walk by their side. Second, when physically restrained during "training," even though the dog may grudgingly mope by your side when "handcuffed" on leash, let's see what happens when she is off leash. History! The dog is in the next county because she never enjoyed walking with you on leash and you have no control over her off leash. So let's just teach the dog

A Siberian Husky demonstrates the proper way to heel.

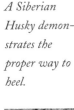

82

off leash from the outset to want to walk with us. Third, if the dog has not been trained to heel, it is a trifle hasty to think about punishing the poor dog for making mistakes and breaking heeling rules she didn't even know existed. This is simply not fair! Surely, if the dog had been adequately taught how to heel, she would seldom make mistakes and hence there would be no need to correct the dog. Remember, each mistake and each correction (punishment) advertise the trainer's inadequacy, not the dog's. The dog is not stubborn, she is not stupid and she is not bad. Even if she were, she would still require training, so let's train her properly.

Let's teach the dog to enjoy following us and to want to walk by our side off leash. Then it will be easier to teach high-precision off-leash heeling patterns if desired. Before going on outdoor walks, it is necessary to teach the dog not to pull. Then it becomes easy to teach on-leash walking and heeling because the dog already wants to walk with you, she is familiar with the desired walking and heeling positions and she knows not to pull.

This Husky and owner maintain good eye contact during training.

83

FOLLOWING

Start by training your dog to follow you. Many puppies will follow if you simply walk away from them and maybe click your fingers or chuckle. Adult dogs may require additional enticement to stimulate them to follow, such as a training lure or, at the very least, a lively trainer. To teach the dog to follow: (1) keep walking and (2) walk away from the dog. If the dog attempts to lead or lag, change pace; slow down if the dog forges too far ahead, but speed up if she lags too far behind. Say "Steady!" or "Easy!" each time before you slow down and "Quickly!" or "Hustle!" each time before you speed up, and the dog will learn to change pace on cue. If the dog lags or leads too far, or if she wanders right or left, simply walk quickly in the opposite direction and maybe even run away from the dog and hide.

Remember, following has a lot to do with attitude—your attitude! Most probably your dog will not want to follow Mr. Grumpy Troll with the personality of wilted lettuce. Lighten up—walk with a jaunty step, whistle a happy tune, sing, skip and tell jokes to your dog and she will be right there by your side.

BY YOUR SIDE

It is smart to train the dog to walk close on one side or the other—either side will do, your choice. When walking, jogging or cycling, it is generally bad news to have the dog suddenly cut in front of you. In fact, I train my dogs to walk "By my side" and "Other side"—both very useful instructions. It is possible to position the dog fairly accurately by looking to the appropriate side and clicking your fingers or slapping your thigh on that side. A precise positioning may be attained by

holding a training lure, such as a chew toy, tennis ball, or food treat. Stop and stand still several times throughout the walk, just as you would when window shopping or meeting a friend. Use the lure to make sure the dog slows down and stays close whenever you stop.

When teaching the dog to heel, we generally want her to sit in heel position when we stop. Teach heel position at the standstill and the dog will learn that the default heel position is sitting by your side (left or right—your choice, unless you wish to compete in obedience trials, in which case the dog must heel on the left).

Several times a day, stand up and call your dog to come and sit in heel position—"Fido, heel!" For example, instruct the dog to come to heel each time there are commercials on TV, or each time you turn a page of a novel, and the dog will get it in a single evening.

Practice straight-line heeling and turns separately. With the dog sitting at heel, teach her to turn in place. After each quarter-turn, half-turn or full turn in place, lure the dog to sit at heel. Now it's time for short straight-line heeling sequences, no more than a few steps

84

at a time. Always think of heeling in terms of sit-heel-sit sequences—start and end with the dog in position and do your best to keep her there when moving. Progressively increase the number of steps in each sequence. When the dog remains close for 20 yards of straight-line heeling, it is time to add a few turns and then sign up for a happy-heeling obedience class to get some advice from the experts.

NO PULLING ON LEASH

You can start teaching your dog not to pull on leash anywhere—in front of the television or outdoors—but regardless of location, you must not take a single step with tension in the leash. For a reason known only to dogs, even just a couple of paces of pulling on leash is intrinsically motivating and diabolically rewarding. Instead, attach the leash to the dog's collar, grasp the other end firmly with both hands held close to your chest, and stand still—do not budge an inch. Have somebody watch you with a stopwatch to time your progress, or else you will never believe this will work and so you will not even try the exercise, and

your shoulder and the dog's neck will be traumatized for years to come.

Stand still and wait for the dog to stop pulling, and to sit and/or lie down. All dogs stop pulling and sit eventually. Most take only a couple of minutes; the all-time record is 22 ½ minutes. Time how long it takes. Gently praise the dog when she stops pulling, and as soon as she sits, enthusiastically praise the dog and take just one step forward, then immediately stand still. This single step usually demonstrates the ballistic reinforcing nature of pulling on leash; most dogs explode to the end of the leash, so be prepared for the

This well-trained Siberian Husky doesn't lead her owner out for a walk. Instead she calmly waits by the door for her owner's directive to go outside.

Training your Siberian Husky will improve the quality of her life.

strain. Stand firm and wait for the dog to sit again. Repeat this half a dozen times and you will probably notice a progressive reduction in the force of the dog's one-step explosions and a radical reduction in the time it takes for the dog to sit each time.

As the dog learns "Sit we go" and "Pull we stop," she will begin to walk forward calmly with each single step and automatically sit when you stop. Now try two steps before you stop. Wooooooo! Scary! When the dog has mastered two steps at a time, try for three. After each success, progressively increase the number of steps in the sequence: try four steps and then six, eight, ten and twenty steps before stopping. Congratulations! You are now walking the dog on leash.

CHAPTER NINE

Resources

BOOKS

About Siberian Huskies

Jennings, Michael. *The New Complete Siberian Husky.* New York: Howell Book House, 1992.

Mentoff, Alexei. *Guide to Owning a Siberian Husky.* Neptune, NJ: TFH Publications, 1996.

Wilcox, Charlotte. *The Siberian Husky.* Minneapolis: Capstone Press, 1999.

About Health Care

American Kennel Club. *American Kennel Club Dog Care and Training.* New York: Howell Book House, 1991.

Carlson, Delbert, DVM, and James Giffen, MD. *Dog Owner's Home Veterinary Handbook.* New York: Howell Book House, 1992.

DeBitetto, James, DVM, and Sarah Hodgson. *You & Your Puppy.* New York: Howell Book House, 1995.

Lane, Marion. *The Humane Society of the United States Complete Guide to Dog Care.* New York: Little, Brown & Co., 1998.

McGinnis, Terri. *The Well Dog Book.* New York: Random House, 1991.

Schwartz, Stephanie, DVM. *First Aid for Dogs: An Owner's Guide to a Happy Healthy Pet.* New York: Howell Book House, 1998.

Volhard, Wendy and Kerry L. Brown. *The Holistic Guide for a Healthy Dog.* New York: Howell Book House, 1995.

About Training

Ammen, Amy. *Training in No Time.* New York: Howell Book House, 1995.

Arden, Andrea. *Train Your Dog The Lazy Way.* New York: Howell Book House, 1999.

Benjamin, Carol Lea. *Mother Knows Best.* New York: Howell Book House, 1985.

Bohnenkamp, Gwen. *Manners for the Modern Dog.* San Francisco: Perfect Paws, 1990.

Dunbar, Ian, Ph.D., MRCVS. *Dr. Dunbar's Good Little Book.* James & Kenneth Publishers, 2140 Shattuck Ave. #2406, Berkeley, CA 94704. (510) 658-8588. Order from Publisher.

Dunbar, Ian. *How to Teach an Old Dog New Tricks.* Oakland: James & Kenneth Publishers, 1998.

Evans, Job Michael. *People, Pooches and Problems.* New York: Howell Book House, 1991.

Palika, Liz. *All Dogs Need Some Training.* New York: Howell Book House, 1997.

Pryor, Karen. *Don't Shoot the Dog.* New York: Bantam Doubleday Dell, 1999.

Volhard, Jack and Melissa Bartlett. *What All Good Dogs Should Know: The Sensible Way to Train.* New York: Howell Book House, 1991.

About Activities

Hall, Lynn. *Dog Showing for Beginners.* New York: Howell Book House, 1994.

O'Neil, Jackie. *All About Agility.* New York: Howell Book House, 1998.

Simmons-Moake, Jane. *Agility Training, The Fun Sport for All Dogs.* New York: Howell Book House, 1991.

Vanacore, Connie. *Dog Showing: An Owner's Guide.* New York: Howell Book House, 1990.

Volhard, Jack and Wendy. *The Canine Good Citizen.* New York: Howell Book House, 1994.

MAGAZINES

THE AKC GAZETTE, The Official Journal for the Sport of Purebred Dogs
American Kennel Club
260 Madison Ave.
New York, NY 10016
www.akc.org

DOG FANCY
Fancy Publications
3 Burroughs
Irvine, CA 92618
(714) 855-8822
http://dogfancy.com

DOG WORLD
Maclean Hunter Publishing Corp.
500 N. Dearborn, Ste. 1100
Chicago, IL 60610
(312) 396-0600
www.dogworldmag.com

PETLIFE: Your Companion Animal Magazine
Magnolia Media Group
1400 Two Tandy Center
Fort Worth, TX 76102
(800) 767-9377
www.petlifeweb.com

DOG & KENNEL
7-L Dundas Circle
Greensboro, NC 27407
(336) 292-4047
www.dogandkennel.com

MORE INFORMATION ABOUT SIBERIAN HUSKIES

National Breed Club

SIBERIAN HUSKY CLUB OF AMERICA, INC.

Corresponding Secretary:
Fain Zimmerman
210 Madera Dr.
Victoria, TX 77905
Sledog@tisd.net

Breeder Contact:
Brenda Rosebrick
20915 NE 169th St.
Brush Prairie, WA 98606
(708) 687-5447
tpaws@pacifier.com

Breed Rescue:
Garry Dalakian
(908) 782-2089

The Club can send you information on all aspects of the breed including the names and addresses of breed clubs in your area, as well as obedience clubs. Inquire about membership.

The American Kennel Club

The American Kennel Club (AKC), devoted to the advancement of pure-bred dogs, is the oldest and largest registry organization in this country. Every breed recognized by the AKC has a national (parent) club. National clubs are a great source of information on your breed. The affiliated clubs hold AKC events and use AKC rules to hold performance events, dog shows, educational programs, health clinics and training classes. The AKC staff is divided between offices in New York City and Raleigh, North Carolina. The AKC has an excellent web site that provides information on the organization and all AKC-recognized breeds. The address is **www.akc.org**.

For registration and performance events information, or for customer service, contact:

THE AMERICAN KENNEL CLUB
5580 Centerview Dr., Suite 200
Raleigh, NC 27606
(919) 233-9767

The AKC's executive offices and the AKC Library (open to the public) are at this address:

THE AMERICAN KENNEL CLUB
260 Madison Ave.
New York, NY 10016
(212) 696-8200 (general information)
(212) 696-8246 (AKC Library)
www.akc.org

UNITED KENNEL CLUB
100 E. Kilgore Rd.
Kalamazoo, MI 49001-5598
(616) 343-9020
www.ukcdogs.com

AMERICAN RARE BREED ASSOCIATION
9921 Frank Tippett Rd.
Cheltenham, MD 20623
(301) 868-5718 (voice or fax)
www.arba.org

CANADIAN KENNEL CLUB
89 Skyway Ave., Ste. 100
Etobicoke, Ontario
Canada M9W 6R4
(416) 675-5511
www.ckc.ca

ORTHOPEDIC FOUNDATION
FOR ANIMALS (OFA)
2300 E. Nifong Blvd.
Columbia, MO 65201-3856
(314) 442-0418
www.offa.org/

Trainers

Animal Behavior & Training Associates
(ABTA)
9018 Balboa Blvd., Ste. 591
Northridge, CA 91325
(800) 795-3294
www.Good-dawg.com

Association of Pet Dog Trainers
(APDT)
(800) PET-DOGS
www.apdt.com

National Association of Dog
Obedience Instructors (NADOI)
729 Grapevine Highway, Ste. 369
Hurst, TX 76054-2085
www.kimberly.uidaho.edu/nadoi

Associations

Delta Society
P.O. Box 1080
Renton, WA 98507-1080
(Promotes the human/animal bond
through pet-assisted therapy and other
programs)
www.petsforum.com/
DELTASOCIETY/dsi400.htm

Dog Writers Association of America
(DWAA)
Sally Cooper, Secretary
222 Woodchuck Lane
Harwinton, CT 06791
www.dwaa.org

National Association for Search and
Rescue (NASAR)
4500 Southgate Place, Ste. 100
Chantilly, VA 20157
(703) 222-6277
www.nasar.org

Therapy Dogs International
6 Hilltop Rd.
Mendham, NJ 07945

OTHER USEFUL RESOURCES— WEB SITES

General Information— Links to Additional Sites, On-Line Shopping

www.k9web.com – resources for the dog
world

www.netpet.com – pet related products,
software and services

www.apapets.com – The American Pet
Association

www.dogandcatbooks.com – book
catalog

www.dogbooks.com – on-line bookshop

www.animal.discovery.com/ – cable
television channel on-line

Health

www.avma.org – American Veterinary Medical Association (AVMA)

www.aplb.org – Association for Pet Loss Bereavement (APLB)—contains an index of national hot lines for on-line and office counseling.

www.netfopets.com/AskTheExperts. html – veterinary questions answered on-line.

Breed Information

www.bestdogs.com/news/ – newsgroup

www.cheta.net/connect/canine/breeds/ – Canine Connections Breed Information Index